Centering Pura Vida

Centering Pura Vida

What it looks like to include the voice
and experience of students of color
in higher education leadership,
diversity, and inclusion programs

Lily E. Espinoza

ABOOKS
Alive Book Publishing

Contents

Dedicated to those who never give up and keep smiling
for themselves and for those around them!

Three Little Birds
by Bob Marley

Rise up this morning, smiled with the rising sun
Three little birds pitch by my doorstep
Singing sweet songs of melodies pure and true
Saying, "This is my message to you-ou-ou"

Preface

When you turn 50 years old, it is a funny time. You have earned a special place in society as an elder. You have a lifetime of experience and memories that provide you with perspective and understanding that only comes with the many trips around the sun. At the same time, you wonder if you are truly a grown up at all. You remember like it was yesterday that feeling of being 10 years old and riding your scooter down Suicide Hill. What can one truly know and understand after 50 years on earth?

I thought about many ways that I could celebrate turning 50 years old, being so fortunate to reach such a milestone. It is truly an honor and one worthy of commemoration. So for me, I decided to put this book together of some of my experiences of working over 20 years in the field of higher education.

There is an old saying of "do what you love, and you will never work a day in your life." Oh, how that has been a foundation of my work!

I used to hear stories of people hating their job, and hearing about the "daily grind" and the Rat Race. I often thought to myself, well, that does not apply to me! Lucky for me, I found my calling. I felt like one of the luckiest people because I was able to work in education.

I found what I loved to do quite by happenstance. I remember being a student at a community college. I was preparing to transfer out because I was admitted to University of California, Berkeley to major in Women's Studies. It was my last semester at the community college. One day I decided to visit the college's Office of Human Resources to see what jobs there were at the college. I thought it would be amazing to work at a community college as a career.

At the Human Resources office there was a binder full of open positions at the college. I found the page that listed the open position of Vice President of Institutional Effectiveness. I read over the job duties and responsibilities. The role ignited my imagination and curiosity. You mean to tell me that it someone's job to study the college operations and student success outcomes? I was hooked! I wanted to do that! I asked for a copy of the job announcement and kept it with me for years as an inspiration.

There I was, someone who only recently turned 20 years old. I had barely graduated from high school. I transferred from community college by the skin of my teeth. Yet, I found my dream job – to serve as a Vice President of Institutional Effectiveness at a community college, and then to become a college president. That moment felt magical and exciting, as if sirens had sounded off: TARGET AQUIRED! I saw my future in the crosshairs. I had found what I was meant to do with my life! I knew instantly that I wanted to dedicate myself to working at the community college for my career. I wanted to be someone who made sure that students did not fall through the cracks. I wanted to be that person who makes sure institutional resources were utilized directly on student success efforts. That programs, services, funding, and facilities were geared toward students first. The job announcement had a minimum qualification of a doctorate preferred and I knew that was my destiny as well. But first I needed to transfer to University of California, Berkeley and actually graduate with a bachelor's degree! Easy peasy!

Now these 20 odd years later, I am so amused with my

younger self. She had stars in her eyes. She thought if she simply followed all the right steps, then she would realize her dream of becoming a college president as easy as 1-2-3. But life does not work out that way. Little did I know but I would experience many career hiccups, campus reorganizations, layoffs, budget cuts, contract cancellations, and involuntary career pivots that I never anticipated. Even so, I have loved every day I could in my work in higher education. It has been a dream come true, working with students to help them in their journey through the higher education maze.

This book is a collection of research, reflections, and stories of my time working in education these last 20 years. These chapters represent lessons learned and examples of ways we can better serve and financially support students of color in diversity and inclusion programs in higher education. I have spent a lifetime doing just that to my utter joy. It has been a wonderful honor. I consider this book my swan song, for I am not sure where the next chapter of my career will lead. Yet I know that I will continue to enjoy *pura vida* in all that I do! Here's to 50 more years!

Lily E. Espinoza
California
2024

Introduction

What exactly is *"pura vida?"* The direct translation means "simple life" or "pure life." The saying is now commonly known as emblematic of the philosophy of a simple, cheerful outlook and lifestyle. There was a Mexican film called Pura Vida from 1956 that made the phrase popular. The phrase has come to symbolize a philosophy of the joy of the simple life. Costa Rica is where the saying *pura vida* captures its essence and the phrase is often said in greeting, in farewell, or as a way to simply acknowledge life as it happens. It is similar to the notion of *"aloha"* in Hawaiian culture. The philosophy celebrates a lifestyle that is relaxed, carefree and optimistic.

I use the phrase "centering *pura vida*" for the book title as a method to pass along what has helped me in my 20 years of experience working in higher education. Centering this philosophy in everyday decisions helps to clear away distractions from the mission by including the voice and experience of students of color in higher education leadership, diversity, and inclusion programs. It comes down to remembering that what works well for students of color, will work well for all students to be successful. Remembering to center the experience of students of color in our policy, practices, and programs lifts the entire student body. Keeping this phrase close to your heart, will allow for you to find clarity and hope for the students who are to come in the future. As the college student demographics continue to shift, our colleges, programs, and resources must change and adapt as well.

This book is made up of four parts and a list of references for someone starting out in a student affairs career in the field of higher education. I start the book by sharing my personal story of how I was able to transfer from a community college to the University of California, Berkeley, which is my professional origins story. To show you how it all started and where my passion to serve came from through my lived experience. It was a story that I have shared over my career. I have used it as the foundation for my dissertation study on Latina transfer students. It is basically my professional origin story for my career in student affairs. If I had not gone to a community college or transferred to UC Berkeley or found the support and love from my peers, professors, and counselors to be successful as a young college student, I may never have found my life's passion. My origin story lays the foundation for my entire career. If I had not had those experiences and that level of support, I may not have ever dedicated myself to working in education. I present that chapter as a starting point for my career and how and why I chose to work and pursue this field as a profession.

The second part of the book is about learning the ropes of student affairs and what student-centered programming and evaluation in higher education should look like. I have worked at various 2-year and 4-year colleges and universities both on the west coast and the east coast. Diversity, inclusion, and belonging programming has been around since the 1960's and the Civil Rights Era that expanded college access to more people of color and non-traditional students in higher education. Over the course of the last 50 years, there have been varying types of programs and services that are dynamic in size and funding. But what every institution has always grappled with is in understanding and measuring the impact and effectiveness of these programs. In Chapter 3, I include a completed program review template that is commonly used for state funded programs that must also include a comprehensive site visit to evaluate funding of support diversity efforts. I was responsible with compiling this narrative report with a team in my department that describes what type of services, counseling, events, courses, and staffing is necessary to run a successful DEI program. As more of these DEI programs come under scrutiny for their return on investment to the college, this program review model can provide some parameters on how to articulate program impacts to the broader community.

For the third part of the book, I provide some lessons learned as I advanced in my career and transitioned from classified staff member to a manager within student affairs. In Chapter 4, I provide a case study of students who filed a grievance complaint against me when I was serving as the Interim Director in a diversity program. I reflect on ways that the situation could have been avoided. I follow that with Chapter 5 which is a discussion on state funding for specific diversity programs in California community colleges. These programs demonstrate academic components that show positive impact on student outcomes, yet each year they are challenged with state budget cuts. In Chapter 6, I analyze the institutionalization of a diversity office on campus that received seed money through a grant from the United States Department of Education to support diversity efforts. There is an analysis of the efforts proposed in the initial grant application, the scope of work of the center, and the operations of the final project that remains at the college to this day.

The final part of the book is about ways to incorporate the philosophy of *pura vida* into the daily work and your vision of leadership to support the success of students of color in higher education. The Code of Ethics in Chapter 7 incorporates standard ethic practices from student-centered professional associations and then a more personalized list of codes based on my years of experience. The next chapter are the voices of students of color who participated in a focus group for my dissertation on Latina student success. I included the raw data and transcribed notes for those interested in pursuing research or those preparing a dissertation on transfer student success. Hearing directly from the students we serve should be the start and end point when it comes to a career in student affairs. These notes highlight the importance of support programs such as the honors program and counselors and the impact of professors who demonstrated that they care. The final chapter is Chapter 9 on the vision I see for the next 50 years of Latinidad in Higher Education. By then, I would imagine every campus in the University of California system would qualify as a Hispanic Serving Institute (HSI), just as most of the community colleges now do. But I provide a helpful leadership model that can be used to develop goals and programs to better serve all students in the higher education pathway.

As I reflect back on my career and experiences over these last twenty years, I am heartened to see a new crop of leaders become college presidents and university leaders. I wish that all these new leaders will go in with *pura vida* and excitement for the future that is yet to come. *Pura vida*!

My Professional Origin Story

My Polish father had a middle-class upbringing in a small town called Waterbury in the state of Connecticut. He was very successful in high school and attended a prestigious private university in New York City before completing his law degree. He used to tell a funny story of how he was admitted to Harvard University through deferred admission, but he turned them down because he did not want to start college in the spring term. My Mexican mother, from a poor family with eight siblings, dropped out of secondary school to immigrate to the United States at the age of sixteen. My mom and dad were both very independent; both of my parents left family and friends to establish a new life in California. When it came to education in my family, it was either sink or swim. I grew up with three sisters and a brother. Each child was individually responsible for his or her own education, and little direction was provided by either my mother or father. Because of my dad's experience in higher education, I had a vague understanding of college admission requirements.

Attending college was always a goal of mine. Even so, I struggled with school. I took Algebra in eighth grade to get a head start on math requirements for college. I failed the class the first time around so I took it again in summer school in order to pass. I took Geometry my first year of high school. Again, I failed the class on the first go around, but passed it during summer school. I moved on to Algebra II and followed the same pattern. I received no intervention from teachers, my parents, counselors, or friends. I never once asked for help from the school, because I did not know how or whom to ask for help.

I had a slightly better time in meeting language requirements. I took a foreign language, Spanish, in junior high school. After completing the required second year of the language, I completed the minimum foreign language requirement by my first year of high school. I even registered for and completed English requirements that were considered "college preparation." I was taking college-track classes but I did not have a clue about how to be a competent student. I felt like an impostor taking college preparation classes, all the while earning sub-standard grades of C's and D's. I had no idea how to take notes in class or how to complete an outline for a paper, and studying was always an afterthought. By my junior year in high school, my grade point average was below 2.0 on a 4.0-point scale. During my senior year in high school, I realized that my low grades made it impossible for me to apply to any four-year university. I felt defeated.

Instead of completing college applications, I found myself struggling to graduate from high school. Because of excessive unexcused absences, I lost high school credits and had to attend night school at the local adult education center to earn enough credits to graduate with my class. One semester after receiving my report card filled with D's and F's, my dad typed onto my report card that I was "doomed to failure" if I kept up the horrible grades. My senior year in high school, I decided not to apply to a university; I figured I did not have a chance of acceptance.

After barely graduating from high school, I realized my only chance to earn a baccalaureate degree would be to transfer from a community college to a university. Even with my terrible academic record, I had academic aspirations of graduating from a top-notch higher educational institution. It was my fantasy to attend a prestigious university. In my eyes, UC Berkeley was at the top of the list. I had a sister who was attending UC Berkeley. She was the star student in the family. My dad saw her potential early on and sent her to the East Coast to attend one of the nation's premier private academies. She chose to start her higher education at UC Berkeley. My sister heard about a community college in the area that had a high transfer rate of students who gained admission to UC Berkeley. She told me about it and I knew that was the answer for me. I sent away for the college catalog and began planning a life in a new location.

Growing up in southern California, the idea of going 400 miles to attend a community college in the San Francisco Bay Area felt like going to another planet. I took a preliminary trip with my father to visit the community college campus and to submit my application, register for classes, and find housing. During that short visit, I realized that the community college was the perfect option for me.

Looking back, I see that the college campus provided me with a comprehensive transfer culture. From completing the community college application to the orientation, I felt the staff and faculty respected my goal to transfer. I felt validated by the college. I completed the recommended college orientation class to learn about transfer eligibility requirements, the transfer curriculum, and transfer services on campus. I learned how to plan for transfer success and received a student handbook to help me understand time management, common college terminology, student services on campus, and other useful resources. I learned about associate degree requirements and made completing an associate degree part of my plan.

When I returned from that trip, I knew that this was the second chance I needed to realize my goals of attaining a bachelor's degree. In addition, I felt that transferring to UC Berkeley was not just a fantasy, but that it could become my reality. Being a risk taker, I felt this was the perfect plan for me. It was the second chance I needed to succeed. At the age of seventeen, I left my hometown and traveled 400 miles to the San Francisco Bay Area.

During my first semester at the community college, I knew that I had found my niche. I found myself awakened to limitless possibilities in my education. I was excited about my classes and made real connections with other students and with the faculty. For the first time, I was eager to go to class and I was engaged in the instructional material. The courses in Women's Studies fascinated me from the start. I found myself getting strong grades and getting involved in campus life, joining clubs and attending campus activities. For the first time, I was earning A's and B's and made the Dean's list during my first year.

While at the community college, life on my own was far from perfect. I hit a few rough patches. The most devastating event occurred my first semester away from home when my father suffered a debilitating stroke, which affected my financial and emotional support. This event forced me to take on a full-time sales position at the local mall to make rent each month. In addition, I failed to realize the importance of applying for financial aid. It took me a few semesters to understand the process to receive federal funding for my education.

One semester, the strain of working full-time and going

to school full-time proved too much, so I returned home to save money. Back home, I enrolled at the local community college and continued to work so I could save enough money to return to the Bay Area. I was committed to return to the community college that gave me the motivation to pursue my dream of transferring to UC Berkeley. After one semester away, I returned to the Bay Area. Upon my return, I was committed to making my transfer plans come true.

Unfortunately, my personal life began to affect my transfer plans. I found myself taking unnecessary risks. I became involved in a personal relationship that was controlling and oppressive. I would miss classes to spend time in the relationship. I was dropping classes and wasting my financial aid funding on poor choices. Because of my risky behavior, I suffered medical problems that affected my coursework. I felt my goal of transferring to UC Berkeley slipping through my fingers, yet I did not have the personal strength to do anything about it. Once again, I felt helpless. My involvement in my relationship isolated me from supportive friends and mentors. Eventually, my grades began to suffer and my grade point average went from a 3.75 to a 3.0.

When it came time to apply to transfer, I was at a low point in my personal life. I had no money for the application when it came time to complete university applications. Stuck in an unhealthy relationship, I felt miserable. I thought that I had no one to turn to for financial assistance. The cost to submit an admission's application to the four-year university ranged from $40 to over $100 per application. To apply to one University of California (UC) campus, the cost was $55. I was living paycheck to paycheck and $55 felt like a large amount of money. The cost to apply to the California State University (CSU) system was $40 per application.

I made the decision to apply to San Francisco State University (SFSU). I barely had the motivation to apply to even one school. The years I spent dreaming about going to UC Berkeley seemed like a distant memory. My dream was not enough for me to commit $55 for the application. I did not apply to UC Berkeley because I did not believe I would get accepted and I did not have the money to gamble on a far-fetched dream. I simply did not believe in myself. Besides, it was cheaper to apply to SFSU and I felt I had a good chance of getting in there. Despite all my academic preparation, aspirations, and commitment, I was foreclosing on my dream.

Fortunately for me, fate stepped in when I needed it the most. One day after I sent in my application to SFSU, by pure happenstance I decided to walk by the Transfer Center at my community college. That day I met someone who changed the direction of my life. The period to file applications was not yet over. There was a representative from UC Santa Cruz sitting at a table recruiting students. I decided to strike up a conversation with the representative. I mentioned that it was a dream of mine to apply to the UC system that I had dreamt of attending UC Berkeley for years. The representative asked me why I did not submit my application. Feeling full of shame and embarrassment, I told him that I did not have the money for the cost of the application and that I did not think I could gain admission. He asked me a few simple questions about the number of siblings I have in my family and about my parent's income. After I told him that I came from a low-income household and that I was one of five children in the family, he explained that I was qualified to receive a UC Application Fee Waiver. The representative from UC Santa Cruz handed me what looked like a certificate, a UC Application Fee Waiver. The fee waiver made it possible for me to apply to three campuses in the UC system free of charge. I could not believe my good luck! I felt like the character Charlie Bucket from the movie *Charlie and the Chocolate Factory* when he found the golden ticket!

There were only a few days left to meet the UC application deadline. In a few days, I had to find two faculty members who would write me letters of recommendation. In addition, I had to complete a personal statement. I was able to find two instructors from my Women's Studies classes who were willing to help me. I used the poem from the student handbook I received during my first-year orientation to inspire me for my personal statement. I put all the materials together for the UC application along with the UC Fee Waiver certificate and sent it off in the mail. I was able to apply to UC Berkeley, UC Santa Cruz, and UC San Diego. I had no idea if I would receive an admission offer to any of those schools. Little did I know, but I would gain admission to each school that I applied to that year.

One by one, the offers of admission began to arrive. The first school to reply was San Francisco State University. I received a postcard telling me that I gained admission as a junior level transfer with a major of Sociology. The next school to contact me was UC Santa Cruz. With great fanfare, they sent a large packet in the mail with a beautiful proclamation of my admission to the campus. The next campus was UC San Diego. They sent a formal letter admitting me to the Thurgood Marshall School for the fall semester. Finally, I received a large packet from my dream school, UC Berkeley. What a happy day!

After my initial exhilaration, I realized that the letter was not exactly what I had hoped. I received deferred admission, just like my dad! They were offering me admission to the spring semester instead of the fall semester, due to the heavy competition of the application pool for the fall semester. To me, this event signaled how precarious my chances of admission were for that university. Being that this event occurred in 1995, the year before the passage of Proposition 209, which ended affirmative action in university admission practices in California, I now understand that I was an affirmative action admit. Yet, going to my dream school one semester late was not going to deter me from transferring to UC Berkeley. I did not hesitate for one minute as I sent in my Statement of Intent to Register (SIR) to UC Berkeley. All I knew was that I was making my dream of transferring to Berkeley a reality!

My admission to UC Berkeley triggered my interest in the decision of other Latina community college students to pursue higher education beyond the two-year college to the four-year university; this interest has led me to my career path. Even before I transferred from the community college, I knew I wanted to work at a community college to promote these wonderful institutions for students such as myself, students who needed a second chance. I saw a potential career working with students to help them transfer from the community college to a university.

After earning my bachelor's degree, I researched career options and learned the job qualifications for working in administration at a community college. I wanted to gain a position of influence in higher education policy. At this time, I was living on the East Coast and exploring graduate programs. Eventually, I learned about graduate programs in the area of higher education administration. This time around,

I had the financial resources to apply to the schools of my choice. Feeling confident after earning a baccalaureate degree from a flagship institution and making the decision to live in New York City, I applied to master's degree programs at New York University and Columbia University. I was eager to experience a private school education at a nationally recognized university. I received offers of admission from both institutions. Lured by the Community College Research Center (CCRC) and the Ivy League name, I chose to attend Teachers College, Columbia University. I completed a master's degree in Student Personnel Administration within the Higher Education Administration program. After completing my degree, I left New York to seek work at a California community college. Shortly afterwards, I accepted my first professional position working as a student services coordinator at a Transfer Center at a community college in the San Francisco Bay Area. I felt like my life had come full circle.

I was fortunate to advance in my career to eventually serve as the director of a Transfer Center at a California community college. It was my dream job, working to build awareness of the transfer options for community college students and to demystify the transfer process. I have always served as an advocate for students who face personal, financial, and social challenges that affect their academic success.

Now, as a professional in the field of higher education for over twenty years, I see the impact of legislation such as Proposition 209 on university admissions policy, and that of Proposition 13 and Proposition 98 on funding in higher education in the state of California. In addition, I see the public scrutiny of the issue of college choice and admission to elite and flagship institutions for underrepresented students.

I work with policy makers and attend professional conferences to lend my voice to the conversations affecting the success of community college students. There are many stories
like mine about students lost in the college pathway, students who have the potential to succeed. As a leader in community college education, my hope has always been to
challenge higher education institutions to look at the stories
of students to inform policy and practices and to recognize
that this effort is critical to the mandate to support graduation rates of underrepresented students.

A Diversity Program Review Model

DIVERSITY UNIT PLAN

The DIVERSITY UNIT Program established in 1969, identifies three areas of impact to the college: student, program, and institutional impact (see Figure 1). Each section of this report will attempt to address how various program policies and actions affect these three areas. In addition, consideration of external impacts from each one of the areas will show how external factors impact DIVERSITY UNIT.

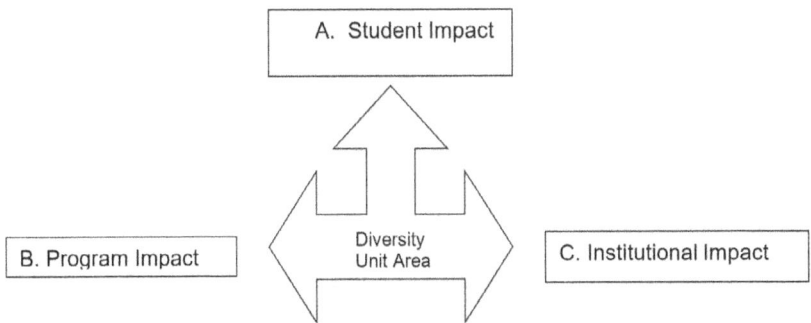

```
                    ┌─────────────────────┐
                    │  A.  Student Impact  │
                    └─────────────────────┘
                              ↑
┌────────────────────┐   ┌──────────┐   ┌──────────────────────────┐
│ B. Program Impact  │ ◄ │ Diversity│ ► │ C. Institutional Impact  │
└────────────────────┘   │ Unit Area│   └──────────────────────────┘
                         └──────────┘
                              ↓
```

Figure 1 - As shown in the above diagram, each area is considered equal in its impact on the college. The diagram illustrates how both internal and external factors affect policy and program planning in the DIVERSITY UNIT program.

A. Student Impact

Two student initiatives, Outreach Initiative and Transfer Initiative have been implemented to address the shift in organizational pedagogy of the program (that is, the shift away from the culture of mediocrity based on traditional indicators of success such as GPA, retention, and enrollment).

The Outreach/Recruitment Initiative will focus on the changing student demographics in the local community and ways to engage more students in the pursuit of higher education. The Outreach/Recruitment Initiative will establish or create college and community partnerships to improve awareness of program services and activities. In addition, in collaboration with campus recruitment, the DIVERSITY UNIT office will offer a series of workshops in the high schools to build better understanding of the college experience akin to summer bridge programs at four-year institutions, which better prepare high school seniors through the transition from high school to college.

The Transfer Initiative will focus on addressing the disparity between achievement and opportunity for academic success. The Transfer Initiative places emphasis on services and activities that improve the transfer rate of DIVERSITY UNIT students through, counseling, workshops, and field trips to four-year institutions. Better utilization of campus resources will provide greater access to information, thereby improving the number of DIVERSITY UNIT students who transfer. In the future, DIVERSITY UNIT will increase activities and services for transfer students to support academic goals through multi-faceted academic, personal, financial, and social programming.

B. Program Impact

DIVERSITY UNIT Program will enhance its curriculum to address this change in pedagogy through various means. The DIVERSITY UNIT program is partnering with the English Department in developing additional learning communities to formulate the DIVERSITY UNIT First Year Experience: a basic skills English course, followed with developmental English, and counseling. In addition, with the hiring of two full-time student services and instructional support coordinators there is the sustained effort on supporting the two aforementioned initiatives. As well, the operation budget for the department has increased over the last three years to reflect the growth in student enrollment, accompanied by increased physical operational space. The office of DIVERSITY UNIT now has better visibility and the opportunity to design a new presence on campus.

C. Institutional Impact

Working with the Research Office, DIVERSITY UNIT will use disaggregated data to better ascertain areas of disparity in overall achievement and retention. The extrapolated data will serve as means to establish programs, advocate for services, initiate discourse on interventions, and improve student engagement. Consistently, research shows that students in DIVERSITY UNIT have a higher level of persistence and enroll in 12 units

or more at a higher rate than does the general East Bay
College student population, proving DIVERSITY UNIT
contribution to the college's FTE numbers. In addition,
DIVERSITY UNIT will continue to work on college-wide
initiatives including the HSI Title V five-year grant and
Community College Campus Change Network.

I. ADVISORY BOARD'S RECOMMENDATIONS

DIVERSITY UNIT has an extensive and representative advisory board which includes members from East
Bay College local community, including student repre-
sentation, feeder institutions, universities and colleges,
government agencies, and non-governmental organizations. The Advisory Board's last meeting took place on
March 31, 2005. As stated in Sections 69648, 69648.7, and
71020 of the California State Education Code, "The Advisory Committee shall meet as least once during each
academic year." In previous meetings, feedback from the
Board was used in planning and implementing new
strategies for student involvement, such as discussing
opportunities to increase communication and providing
outreach services to local feeder schools. Also, the Board
was critical in the discussion of improving recruitment
and retention efforts for the program. DIVERSITY UNIT
promotes the notion of reciprocity with the members of
its board. There are expectations of promoting and providing support for community activities and opportunities for students by all members of the board. In addition,
DIVERSITY UNIT joins with board members on issues
affecting access and the state of education, such as supporting legislation issues and petitioning state represen-

tatives. Specifically, in 2005, because of a recommended action by a board member, DIVERSITY UNIT students took part in a march to the state capital and letter writing campaign to state representatives during proposed state budget cuts to education.

PLAN SUMMARY

First, due to a lack of continuity in advisory meetings, DIVERSITY UNIT will work to re-establish the advisory board meetings to include meaningful agendas and meeting minutes. Next, the Board will work to make a permanent agreement among the members to meet on quarterly basis. To achieve this, the members will discuss their commitment to improving the state of the East Bay College DIVERSITY UNIT program and its contributions to the local community. In addition, in an effort to maximize the resources of its board members, DIVERSITY UNIT will encourage the Board to serve as a working group to support activities that improve the efforts of DIVERSITY UNIT in student retention, intervention, and persistence. Lastly, the Board will now serve as an approving body on changes to policies, practices, and processes within the program.

II. STUDENT LEARNING OUTCOMES

Student Services at East Bay College, including DIVERSITY UNIT, has been working on understanding and clarifying an approach to Student Learning Outcomes (SLO's). The work has been deliberate and intentional as an endeavor to continue cultivating a culture of assessment.

To develop a shared philosophical approach to learning outcomes and assessment, there were two retreats in Spring term, in which the majority of Student Services staff and faculty attended.

Within the institution of East Bay College, SLO's are understood to be defined as statements of expectation that articulate what students will know, do, think, or feel as a result of the students' interaction with program. The SLO's specify how learning will be assessed and document the results of the assessment and how the results will be used to improve learning.

A. Student Impact

With the above stated intentions, the following SLO's have been designed to encompass overarching Student Services goals:

Student Services Institution-Level Learning Outcomes
1. Students will demonstrate proficiency in the use of internet services for personal wellbeing.
2. Students will demonstrate proficiency in self-advocacy.

The first learning outcome, students will demonstrate proficiency in the use of internet services for personal wellbeing, is designed to support student utilization of the increasing number of internet services. Proficiency in using internet services will be essential to students' experiences at East Bay College, when they transfer, and in their life experiences (such as internet banking, internet bill paying, internet tax forms, mental health services, etc.). This learning outcome was approved by the Student Services staff and faculty who attended two retreats. The program implemented a pilot assessment of the SLO in Fall, which is currently under revision.

The second learning outcome, students will demonstrate proficiency in self-advocacy, is designed to help students develop the confidence and capacity to be effective in navigating complex public organizations; these skills will help students facilitate a positive and productive experience while in college, and when they transfer to other educational institutions, and as they work with various private and community agencies. This outcome is also designed to support the development of relationships between students and staff/faculty members that will lead to successful resolution of concerns, attention to grievances, and achievement of goals. For example, when students come to the office asking for information on how to file an appeal, we will help teach them the skills they need to write an appeal that describes their situation, and helps illustrate their circumstances in a concise and acceptable manner. When the appeal is reviewed and subsequently approved/denied, the office response to the appeal will also help teach students about the reasons for the approval/denial. Ultimately, creating intentional processes with the learning outcomes in mind will provide opportunities for reflective and honest critique that allows the office to redefine and create changes within our realm of responsibilities for the program and the college.

B. Program Impact

In conjunction with meeting the first SLO and to expedite the student eligibility process; the DIVERSITY UNIT program is developing an online student application. Giving students the option of completing an online application allows students better access to the program and integrates the SLO of demonstrating proficiency of use of on-line services at the college. Ultimately, the utilization of a digital DIVERSITY UNIT application will allow for the program to enhance students' experience with the program because their application will be processed quickly and free time up used for data entry.

Current DIVERSITY UNIT programming reflects to importance of proficiency in self-advocacy. For example, during the DIVERSITY UNIT student orientation and through counseling contacts, students receive referrals and recommendations to identify sources of support to meet their personal, academic, and financial needs. When students fail to meet program requirements, students have the opportunity to petition to remain in the program though written correspondence.

DIVERSITY UNIT PROGRAM
LEVEL STUDENT LEARNING OUTCOMES

The Student Services SLO's will work in conjunction with the program level SLO's for DIVERSITY UNIT. This structure allows for resources to be consolidated in terms of information gathering as well as for data analysis and in planning. DIVERSITY UNIT has developed program level SLO's to evaluate specific aspects of the program.

DIVERSITY UNIT is a positive learning community that embraces and enhances the cognitive, social, and personal factors of the student's collegiate experience.

A. Student Impact

Because of the unique functions of DIVERSITY UNIT, there are two additional SLO's identified at the program level.

As a result of interacting with this program/completing this program, students achieve the following:
1. DIVERSITY UNIT Students will be able to identify various resources available for social, personal, academic development
2. DIVERSITY UNIT Students will be able to explain the meaning, privileges, and obligations of socially conscientious citizenship

B. Program Impact

DIVERSITY UNIT is framing the language of the Student Learning Outcomes and action to include issues around equity, access, and inclusion within East Bay College. To address these issues, DIVERSITY UNIT began the development of Learning Communities specifically addressing these circumstances. Both the *Create2Change* and *Classroom without Borders* are learning communities that are integral components in developing the DIVERSITY UNIT First Year Experience. Also, there are increased efforts in outreach and intervention with the hiring of two coordinators to focus on these areas. This additional staff has increased the type and scope of workshops and methods of engagement for the DIVER-SITY UNIT students and potential DIVERSITY UNIT students.

Furthermore, DIVERSITY UNIT philosophy supports the development of a multifaceted services program creating an environment characterized by mutual understanding, respect, and care in which students interact and engage with peers, staff, faculty, and the community in the style of a true learning environment.

Examples of programming which support the learning outcomes include:

- Annual Student Empowerment Conference
- Latino Film Festival
- Cinco de Mayo Conference
- Field trips/Excursions
- Counseling Services
- Learning Communities
- Workshops
- Student Orientation
- Recruitment/Information Sessions
- Supporting student activities
- Financial Assistance/Planning
- Priority Registration
- Campus Referrals
- Mutual Responsibility Agreement
- Mid-Semester Progress Report (MSRP)
- Appeal Process

C. Institutional Impact

The development of relevant and responsive DIVERSITY UNIT Student Learning Outcomes is a result of the program's commitment to social justice. It is for these reasons that DIVERSITY UNIT realizes the need for innovation, creativity, and collaboration in all aspects of program development. Lastly, adopting the culture of assessment and evaluation in determining students' needs and program services ensure appropriateness and effectiveness of DIVERSITY UNIT efforts.

PLAN

The learning outcomes will be assessed in the following steps:
1. Identify SLO and develop an Assessment Plan
2. Data Collection
3. Data Analysis and Use of Results
4. Repeat the cycle using results of preliminary SLO's to revise outcomes as needed

A. Program Impact

A survey instrument will be designed and implemented for fall semester to measure the two learning outcomes for the program. With the recommendations of the Student Learning Outcome Advisory Committee, the survey instrument and guidelines will be completed.

B. Institutional Impact

The department will require input from faculty, staff, student workers, and students in the program to complete the assessment. It will be necessary to produce a survey instrument, a means to distribute the survey, and the staff to analyze the results. Having access to the pertinent information from the district database and institutional research will be critical. The college will need to support these data gathering efforts by informing the department on the process of working with the Research Office to improve lines of communications to meet these requirements.

IV. CURRICULUM REVIEW

A. Student Impact

In the course of participating in DIVERSITY UNIT, students have the opportunity to receive services and support that are "above and beyond" those provided by the College for the student population at large. For this reason, the program curriculum is based on reaching underrepresented students and improving their chances for success through innovative and holistic approaches. The DIVERSITY UNIT Program curriculum is designed to address three services areas: Academic, Financial, and Social Support Services.

Students in the DIVERSITY UNIT Program benefit from the following services:

- Personalized Academic Counseling
- Academic Progress Monitoring
- Career & Transfer Exploration. Workshops
- Priority Registration
- Book Vouchers
- Academic Supplies
- Grants/Scholarships
- Transportation Support
- Calculator Loan Program
- FAFSA preparation assistance
- Auxiliary Support

Social Development Activities

DIVERSITY UNIT Conferences

The DIVERSITY UNIT program implemented the annual Student Empowerment Conference to address issues important to DIVERSITY UNIT students. The Student Empowerment Conference was first designed in 2003 to expand students' horizon, self-value, and identity while embracing and enhancing the social factors of students' collegiate experience. The purpose of the conference is to develop positive social communities by creating a space in which individuals can authentically engage in the production and creation of knowledge. It is also a pathway to developing critical thinking, allowing students as well as staff and faculty to formulate a way to think, learn about implicit bias, and distorted, partial, uniformed or prejudiced reasoning. Also, the Student Empowerment Conference aspires to provide discipline and structure to critical thinking and to improve the quality of thoughts, actions, and most importantly results. It has become critical in validating the experience and existence of DIVERSITY UNIT students.

In 2003, DIVERSITY UNIT hosted the first Student Empowerment Conference which placed focus on social issues affecting students including poverty, fair housing, and changing demographics in race and migration. In 2004, the second conference was devoted to issues in Hip Hop, a look at this historical, cultural, social resource for social change. The third Student Empowerment Conference titled, "Awakening of the Mind, Body, and Soul" delved into issues of self-awareness, self-determination, standing against domestic violence, and the sociology of education. In 2006, the fourth annual Student Empowerment Conference, "Liberating Minds...Liberating Society," was a commemoration of the 40th anniversary of the Black Panther Party.

In addition to the Student Empowerment conferences, there have been on-going activities to support DIVERSITY UNIT student social development. In 2005 DIVERSITY UNIT hosted an event entitled "When is Cinco de Mayo this year?: Re-historizing the Past and the Present." In 2004, DIVERSITY UNIT hosted the Latino Film festival. Also, DIVERSITY UNIT sponsors student activities directly related to students served by DIVERSITY UNIT. An example of this support is in fall 2006, DIVERSITY UNIT hosted a Black Student Union Pizza Forum. Lastly, each year DIVERSITY UNIT responds to campus events and changing social climate, by hosting, sponsoring, and promoting activities that support DIVERSITY UNIT student social and academic development.

Excursion/Field Trips

Sunrise Celebration

For the last five years, the DIVERSITY UNIT office has sponsored a trip for students to Alcatraz Island to participate in The Indigenous People's sunrise ceremony. The ceremony is a commemoration of the start of the 1969-1971 occupation of Alcatraz by the "Indians of All Tribes" — an event that galvanized the new indigenous people's rights movement in the United States. The International Indian Treaty Council sponsors the event twice each fall on Alcatraz Island.

Black Panther: Rank & File Exhibit

In anticipation of the 2006 4th Annual Student Empowerment Conference, _Liberty Minds...Liberty Society_, a commemoration of the 40th anniversary of the Black Panther Movement, students visited the Yerba Buena Center for the Arts in San Francisco to observe the "Black Panther Rank and File" Exhibit. The exhibition allowed students to examine how art can be used as a medium to shape society as well as showcasing how art can inspire awareness of critical social concerns. When asked if the exhibit encouraged community activism one student replied, "I try to participate actively with my community, this exhibit made me realize how much it means to me to stay active. I cannot rely on anyone to do it for me. If I want change, I have to make it happen."

B. Program Impact

In an attempt to enhance relations with students and to increase student retention and persistence: the DIVERSITY UNIT Counseling curriculum is developed with avenues to engage students outside the traditional counseling contact. In addition, distinction is made between New (that is first-time participant in DIVERSITY UNIT) and that of Continuing DIVERSITY UNIT students by addressing and accommodating the students based on their involvement with the program and the program expectations specific for new and continuing students.

DIVERSITY UNIT/CARE Counseling Requirements

- All DIVERSITY UNIT/CARE students must have three counseling contacts per semester.
- The contacts must follow a semester-specific timeline to ensure requirements are met in a timely manner.
- The three counseling contacts must be with a DIVERSITY UNIT counselor.

DIVERSITY UNIT Faculty Counseling Philosophy

The DIVERSITY UNIT Counselors at East Bay College are committed to providing authentic and comprehensive support to the academic and social development of our students. Our goal is the promotion of self-awareness, self-determination, and self-reliance to assist our students in navigating through the educational system successfully. This is a shared responsibility between the student and the counselor that promotes initiative and growth in the student. The DIVERSITY UNIT counselors at EBC want to provide support by creating an environment characterized by mutual understanding, respect, and care in which students participate not only in their course work but interact with and engage other students in the style of a true learning community.

New Student Counseling Contacts	Continuing Student Counseling Contacts
Small group Counseling • Exploration/Assessment • Major/Transfer/Career • 2 Semester Ed Plan	**Educational Plan Update***
6 Semester Ed Plan* **Mid-semester Progress Report** • Academic intervention • Letters (satisfactory/unsatisfactory) • Letter from last counselor contact	**Small group Counseling** • Career Exploration • Goal Setting • Time Management **Mid-semester Progress Report and Degree Audit** • Transferring Students • Near 70 Degree Applicable units
Pre-Registration Advising • BOGG • FAFSA	**Pre-registration Advising** **Exit Interview** • BOGG • FAFSA

*Students who are in multiple retention programs (Puente, DSPS, and CalWORKs) must bring in a copy of their educational plans by the DIVERSITY UNIT time guidelines for those requirements to be counted as completed.

Student Counseling Contacts

I. Exploration/Assessment: (1 hour) The purpose is to allow students the opportunity to become acquainted with resources available to help them meet their educational goal

  A. Small group (6-10 students) orientation about transfer and career exploration on the East Bay College campus.

    1. Orientation to include an exploration of materials, technology, and services available to the students.

    2. Students will be encouraged to explore their interests, values, and skills through assessment tools available, such as the Strong Interest Inventory, and the Myers/Briggs Personality Type Inventory.

    3. Students will practice using the Internet and programs such as Eureka to research requirements for careers, college majors available, labor market information. Etc.

  B. Two Semester Educational Plan: Student and Counselor collaborate on planning classes that reflect a students' preliminary educational goal in order to facilitate the academic integration of the student to the educational system.

    1. Using information gathered from Transfer and Career Center orientations, students choose educational goals and possible majors to begin their academic planning.

    2. Student will be reintroduced to IGETC/CSU/AA requirements and the implications they will have on their academic planning. It will also be necessary to review the college catalog with the student. (Materials: College Catalog)

    3. The two semester Educational Plan will be developed in collaboration with a counselor that reflects the students' interests and educational goals.

II. Six Semester Ed Plan (1 hour)

  A. A six semester Ed plan will be developed with a counselor giving students an opportunity to visualize each semester through completion of their goals. When goals are divided into smaller objectives and made specific, the larger goals are more likely to be achieved.

1. Depending on students' educational goal (AA, certificate, IGETC, CSU) begin with planning general education.

2. After further major/university exploration, work with students on major requirements (www.assist.org) as second step in educational plan.

3. One of the final steps is to add transferable elective courses to educational plan.

4. Make sure there are 60 transferable units.

5. Advise student to visit transfer center to plan visits to universities.

B. MSPR (15 minutes) The MSPR provides both students and DIVERSITY UNIT counselors a view of students' progress. It also gives the student an opportunity to discuss progress with his/her instructor. It will serve as an assessment for needed academic interventions that will support the students' success.

1. Counselors can recommend appropriate academic interventions such as individual tutoring, lab assistance, or additional help in the Teaching and Learning Center. Appropriate interventions will be explored to individually help the student. However, it is also the student's responsibility to pursue the interventions.

2. Letters will be sent to students who are not progressing satisfactorily as well as to those who are. "Unsatisfactory" letters indicate that students need to make an appointment with a counselor discuss academic as well as personal issues that may be interfering with

achievement. "Satisfactory" letters acknowledge the student's academic success.

Learning Communities

In addition to the required counseling appointments, students have the opportunity to participate in the learning community, *Classroom without Boarders* at East Bay College, team-taught by an English faculty member, and a DIVERSITY UNIT counselor and the DIVERSITY UNIT Director. Pairing developmental English 70 with counseling Human Services 909, students actively receive instruction in critical development to enhance skill development in English as well as to raise social consciousness.

Classroom without Boarders Philosophy

Classroom without Borders was created to integrate English 70 with Create2Change (Human Services 909) and to form an experience of community and support for students, teachers, tutors and counselor. Classroom without Borders is an opportunity to engage actively in the development of student learning and student consciousness. Learning does not just happen in a classroom but occurs daily in our lives and in the world. Therefore, students are expected to become active and critical producers of culture and not just "mindless consumers."

Components/Expectations

Classroom without Borders courses are linked

purposefully. Students who do not attend both classes will be dropped from the classes. It is expected that students are actively involved in both classes and the tutoring and counseling component. There will be integrated and shared assignments between both classes. Each class will be graded separately but will have common assignments that will be evaluated in final grades.

Course: English 70

English 70 will operate as a reading/writing workshop. Together students read novels, poems, short stories, and essays. Students write informally in journals and write formal summary/responses and essay. In creating written versions and interpretations of, and reactions to the various texts, students will improve reading, writing, and critical thinking skills.

Course: Create2Change (Human Services 909)

This course will be a seminar in which students will use Hip Hop, Spoken Word, Cartooning, and Film to develop a deeper understanding of culture and society. Overall, the class is based on a pedagogical framework to include deconstruction, reconstruction and dialogical action. The "linking" of English 70 with Human Services 909 will promote a deeper understanding of academic and cultural competencies through the development of critical literacy. Critical literacy provides a way to think about and engage in issues that uncover social inequality and injustice.

Tutoring/Study Groups

An integral component of Classroom without Borders will be the integration and availability of tutoring and study groups. All students are expected to participate in both as part of the learning community. Tutoring/Study groups will be integrated in both classes and will be part of the final grade.

Counseling

All students are required to meet with the Classroom without Borders Counselor throughout the semester. There are required appointments to meet with the counselor and to create an educational plan. The counselor will also continuously maintain contact with students. If there is an issue or concern, it is important that students inform the counselor so an adequate intervention or resolution can occur.

PLAN

A. Student Impact

To address the shifting needs of students, each academic year there needs to continue to be a dialogue about student academic and personal needs in the DIVERSITY UNIT curriculum. The services offered continue to be assessed. For example, students received free parking permits this year. Yet, the service was underutilized. The financial resources could have been better allocated to serve a wider audience. One planning objective is to evaluate direct services and their effectiveness. These services can also be evaluated using the Student Learning Outcomes survey instruments to confirm services are relevant.

In addition to the re-evaluation of direct student services, the area of instructional support is under evaluation. The academic performance of the students in DIVERSITY UNIT underscores the objective to devote program resources to better support academic achievement. The data charts in section V. Program Resources and Development of this report, show DIVERSITY UNIT students return semester after semester at a higher rate than the general student population, but that they have a lower rate of retention and show high levels of underperforming in their classes. It is recommended that the DIVERSITY UNIT program advocate for a specific DIVERSITY UNIT tutoring program designed for DIVERSITY UNIT students.

The aim of the DIVERSITY UNIT curriculum is to go "above and beyond" from the traditional classroom experience. The program is designed within the framework that benefit students while supporting their academic, social, and financial needs. Part of that support is the tutoring component, which is critical and must be restored.

Currently, East Bay College offers tutoring services to the general student population. DIVERSITY UNIT tutoring was absorbed into the tutoring services at-large. The data indicate that DIVERSITY UNIT student success is lower than the general student population, demonstrating that DIVERSITY UNIT students require additional academic support.

In addition to providing tutoring services, it is

expected that DIVERSITY UNIT will support auxiliary instructional support services to include:

- Peer Support groups
- Study Groups
- Workshops on communications with faculty, selecting academic mentors, obtaining faculty recommendations, understanding faculty grievance process, understanding course syllabi, time management, study skills, and selecting courses
- Campus student services referrals
- Coordination with academic services on campus i.e. Library, Computer Labs, DSPS, Honors Programs, Business Lab, Math Lab, English Lab, Science Lab and Academic Departments

These efforts to improve academic services throughout the DIVERSITY UNIT program activities align with Student Learning Outcomes for students to identify various resources available for social, personal, academic development as stated earlier in the report.

B. Program Impact

DIVERSITY UNIT First Year Experience

In response to the developmental needs of DIVERSITY UNIT students, the DIVERSITY UNIT First Year Experience is a learning community designed to scaffold students through developmental English courses with "above and beyond" academic, social, and financial support to provide specifically-designed opportunities for success. This effort also supports the Student Learning

Outcomes for the program. In Spring 2007, students will have the opportunity to complete the developmental English sequence, English 70 to English 90 in a DIVERSITY UNIT learning community. Students who complete English 90 meet the reading and writing competency requirements set for Certificate of Achievement at East Bay College. In addition, students who complete English 90 then meet prerequisites for English 100 College Composition, which is the requirement to meet associate degree requirements and minimum transfer requirements.

DIVERSITY UNIT Transfer Initiative

DIVERSITY UNIT program curriculum includes efforts to increasing the transfer rate of DIVERSITY UNIT students by 25-35% beginning Fall 2008. Student persistence and retention is crucial to reach this goal. DIVERSITY UNIT counseling will create intentional interventions to educate, to guide, and to finalize transfer plans with students. Currently, an increase of 5% transfer rate is the standard formula; however, a consistent and continual increase is essential to impact the program's goals of above and beyond.

The Transfer Initiative will categorize students into two groups: Pre-Transfer and Transfer. Each category will have intentional workshops that will be specific to the goals of the population. In conjunction, a scholarship workshop will also be part of the overall information available to students.

In assessing student needs and concerns about transferring two essential components were relevant: knowledge of the process and financial assistance. The Transfer

Initiative aims to demystify these components and provide the intervention needed for successful completion.

Many DIVERSITY UNIT students are first-generation college students without knowledge of the educational system. The known information can be reduced to vocational and certificate programs, as well as AA/AS and the transfer process becomes secondary. The lived realities of many students may catapult them to seek a shortened education, such as an AA degree. The Transfer Initiative hopes to demystify what are the elements of transferring and what the benefits are.

The Transfer and Scholarship workshops will occur before and during the application period for the CSU and UC system. The scholarship workshops will also occur during relevant application time.

Students will be categorized into pre-transfer and transfer ready students. The appropriate correspondence will be sent out in timely manner and the dates and times of workshops will be appropriately advertised. The pre-transfer students are those with 45 units or more and transfer ready students will be at 60 or more units.

EVENT	ACTION	DEADLINE
Transfer and Scholarship workshops	Calendar	August
Correspondence and Advertising	ACCESS query for units Letters	One month before workshops begin
Pre-Transfer workshop	Evaluation	
Transfer/Scholarship		

Transfer/Scholarship

The counseling component continually undergoes transformation to address student needs, for example addition of small group counseling, leaning communities, and better integration of instruction and students services. This effort must continue to be monitored for effectiveness as determined with institutional goals and student learning outcomes. The DIVERSITY UNIT Transfer Initiative is a direct effort geared toward supporting institutional goals and promoting student learning outcomes.

C. Institutional Impact

The DIVERSITY UNIT Program will continue to better utilize institutional research and disaggregated data to pinpoint areas which require formal processes to address shortfalls in the curriculum. This understanding will better enable the DIVERSITY UNIT Program to establish effective intervention measures that are responsive and relevant to current student issues. There needs to be better understanding of current trends in retention and intervention methods used in similar college campus communities. The practices based on successful models need to be evaluated and assessed for potential use in the Program. To address this concern, there is a planned trip to City College of San Francisco with the objective of understanding their student orientation process, which takes place prior to the beginning of the academic year. Also, each year the staff of DIVERSITY UNIT attend the statewide CCCDIVERSITY Conference to keep abreast of current trends and developments for the DIVERSITY UNIT community, as well as other professional development as discussed in the Program Resources and Development section below.

V. PROGRAM RESOURCES AND DEVELOPMENT

REVIEW

A. Student Impact

Program resources have included additions to the program staff which resulted in better delineation of core responsibilities based on new initiatives and program needs. For students, this means the student eligibility process has been streamlined because of the DIVERSITY UNIT Assistant. Also student involvement will improve because two Coordinators have been assigned to specific retention/intervention and outreach/recruitment projects. With the addition of a full-time counselor in 2006 and three part-time counselors, students have the opportunity to offer small group counseling at a variety of times and days of the week. The student employees are invaluable to keeping student files updated and organized, as well as assisting with timely communications with students via telephone, mail, and through in-person interactions.

B. Program Impact

During the 2003 Program Review, the need to hire an Outreach and Retention Specialist was stated. Due to loss of district matching, the position had been eliminated. During Summer 2006, two Student Services and Instructional Support Coordinators were hired on a full-time basis. These two positions are expected to improve outreach and retention efforts for the program. As well, these two coordinators have been appointed to improve the transfer functions and intervention strategies, as stated earlier in the report.

Staffing Trends

DIVERSITY UNIT Staff	2006-2007	2005-2006	2004-2005
Program Manager	1	1	1
Full-time counselors	1	0	0
Part-time counselors	3	4	4
Student Services & Instructional Support Coordinators	2	0	0
DIVERSITY UNIT Assistant	1	.5	.5
CARE Admin. Assistant	.5	.5	0
Student Employees	5	5	5

In fall 2006 there was the addition of a full-time DI-VERSITY UNIT Counselor, in addition to the three part-time counselors, there is better coordination of counseling activities, such as Scholarship/Transfer Workshops and small group counseling appointments. Also, having a full-time counselor provides a means to establish better communication with the Counseling Department, as well as the Transfer Center, Honors Institute, Puente, Outreach, and DSPS. In addition, having a full-time counselor resulted in more opportunities for committee engagement and greater engagement on campus.

Professional Development

Professional development takes place on an on-going basis, as well as in formal yearly events. Each year, the DIVERSITY UNIT staff attends the statewide CCCDI-VERSITY UNITA conference to develop comprehensive understanding of statewide practices. In Fall 2006, the DI-VERSITY UNIT staff designed and presented a seminar on the philosophical approaches to transformative program services to enhance student development and retention. Staff also attends statewide financial aid conferences, namely the CCCSFAA and CASFAA conferences for professional development. Throughout the year, there are opportunities for training to improve technical skills, researching methods, exploring personal interests, and community building activities. Each member of the staff is responsible for attending professional development activities and for articulation professional development needs. In addition, the office holds periodic discussions on office management and work flow support. As well, there are yearly staff retreats to build interpersonal communication skills and to address time management.

C. Institutional Impact

Committee Participation

Participation by the program faculty and staff in various committees is abundant. All members from the staff are encouraged to pursue participation in committee work to enhance professional development, campus community, and to foster better relationships across departments. Through committee participation, DIVERSITY UNIT staff can stay informed of current trends in professional development and practices and contribute on behalf of the office in activities. Detailed below is committee participation by staff in DIVERSITY UNIT.

Committees	Type	Faculty/Manager	Staff
Latina Leadership Network	Statewide	1	0
DIVERSITY UNIT Advisory Board	Region	2	4
Student Learning Outcomes	College	1	1
Chicano/Latino Intersegmental Convocation	Statewide	1	1
Community College Campus Change Network	Statewide	1	1
Umoja Conference Planning Committee	District	1	1
Hispanic Serving Institute	College	2	1
DIVERSITY UNIT Retreat Committee	Department	0	1
Student Empowerment Planning Committee	College	1	2
Program Review Committee	College	0	1
Region III Committee	Statewide	1	0
Scholarship Committees	College	0	1
Hiring Committees	College	2	2
College Success day	College	1	1
Job Fair Committee	College	1	1
Commencement Committee	College	1	0
Tutoring Committee	College	1	0
CalWORKs Association	Statewide	1	1

PLAN

A. Student Impact

The academic performance of the students in DIVERSITY UNIT underscores the objective to devote program resources to better support academic achievement. The data below show DIVERSITY UNIT students return semester after semester at a higher rate than the general student population, but that they have a lower rate of retention and underperforming in their classes. It is recommended that the DIVERSITY UNIT program advocate for a tutoring program specifically for DIVERSITY UNIT students. Currently, East Bay College offers tutoring services to the general student population. DIVERSITY UNIT tutoring was absorbed into the tutoring services at-large. The data indicate that DIVERSITY UNIT student success is lower than the general student population, demonstrating that DIVERSITY UNIT students require additional academic support.

In addition to providing tutoring services, it is expected that DIVERSITY UNIT will support auxiliary academic support services to include:
- Peer Support groups
- Study Groups
- Workshops on communications with faculty, selecting academic mentors, obtaining faculty recommendations, understanding faculty grievance process, understanding course syllabi, time management, study skills, and selecting courses
- Campus student services referrals
- Coordination with academic services on campus i.e. Library, Computer Labs, DSPS, Honors Programs, Business Lab, Math Lab, English Lab, Science Lab and Academic Departments

These efforts to improve academic services throughout the DIVERSITY UNIT program activities align with Student Learning Outcomes for students to identify various resources available for social, personal, academic development as stated earlier in the report.

Retention and Success Rates: Retention rates for Diversity Unit students have been at 19% and 13% for fall semesters and 72 and 71% for spring semesters. Success rates have been at 58% for fall semesters and 54% for spring semesters. When compared to the College average, the retention rate of Diversity Unit students has been higher by about 5% and the success rate has been higher by about 5% also.

C. Institutional Impact

With greater support to the academic, social, and financial support of DIVERSITY UNIT students, this will result in an increase in student retention, increase in FTE's and greater transfer rates. By improving instructional support in the form of learning communities and tutoring, students develop greater sense of engagement with the campus and their peers.

VI. COLLABORATION ACROSS THE ACADEMIC COMMUNITY

REVIEW

Collaboration is integral to the success of the DIVERSITY UNIT Programs. The programs' ability to build capacity in a time resources are constantly diminishing is integral for the sustainability of the DIVERSITY UNIT Program. To deliver efficient and effective student services, DIVERSITY UNIT currently partners with various programs within East Bay College (EBC) such as Puente, DSPS, Child Study Center, Associated Students, Voc. Tech., Outreach, Automotive Center, College Bookstore, Transfer Center, Pathways, English Department, Food Services, etc. The philosophy behind the partnerships is to enhance support services and increase the academic impact services have on students at EBC.

PLAN

In collaboration with various communities (CBO, government, corporate, academic, etc.), DIVERSITY UNIT will develop a funding forum for future programs and services. Such programs include, Student Empowerment Conference, Film Festival, Southern California College Tours, etc. It is for this reason that DIVERSITY UNIT works closely and in conjunction with the EBC Grants Officer, HIS Title V, Foundation Office, Transfer Center, and Associated Students Office.

DIVERSITY UNIT will re-energize relationships with EBC Counseling and Instructional faculty. The relationship is critical in developing counseling and classroom opportunities for students served by DIVERSITY UNIT. Besides counseling services, DIVERSITY UNIT partner with EBC's Fast Track efforts to offer, Summer Access/Bridge projects for potentially eligible DIVERSITY UNIT high school students.

In conjunction with the Marketing Office and Information Technology, DIVERSITY UNIT/CARE will research the possibility of providing more on-line services (application, academic monitoring and college advising).

VII. OTHER PROGRAM ISSUES

Part 1. Diversity Unit Data

Gender: Proportion of females in DIVERSITY UNIT has increased from 66% in fall 2003 to 75% in fall 2005, an increase of 9% points in the last three semesters. Conversely, males have decreased. When compared to the college population, the DIVERSITY UNIT Office serves more females than males.

DIVERSITY UNIT serves a higher number of females over males within DIVERSITY UNIT and in relation to EBC. There needs to be greater recruiting effort geared toward attracting males to participate in the program. This means better marketing and recruiting reflecting men and the development of a male student peer support system.

Ethnicity: African Americans, Hispanics and Whites have been the majority of students receiving services from DIVERSITY UNIT for the last five semesters. African-Americans have increased from 35% in fall 2003 to 38% in fall 2005, an increase of 3% points. Hispanics have decreased by 1% point in the last five semesters. When compared to the college population, DIVERSITY UNIT serves a larger proportion of African-American students.

Age Group: The majority of students in DIVERSITY UNIT are 24 years of age or younger. Students receiving DIVERSITY UNIT services and of 19 years old or younger increased from 28% in fall 2003 29% in fall 2005, a 1% point increase. When compared to the college population, there are slightly more students between the ages of 20-24 receiving DIVERSITY UNIT services.

Overall, the DIVERSITY UNIT program serves a younger age group of students then the campus in general. Services geared toward a younger student need to be considered in the coming years of planning. As well, how the program recruits new students must take into consideration the transition from high school to college. This issue is being addressed in the Outreach Initiative discussed in Section IV. Curriculum.

Educational Objectives: Of those DIVERSITY UNIT students who indicated having an educational objective, most have a long term objective. However, there are a large number of students with undecided and unreported educational objective. When compared to the overall college population, generally more DIVERSITY UNIT students have long-term objectives.

With counseling services as a primary contact with DIVERSITY UNIT students, there should not be such a high number of students with undecided and unreported educational objectives. To address this concern, there needs to be better contact with students about keeping counseling appointments and training with counselors to make sure they are informing students and inputting educational objectives into the proper databases, including MIS, Datatel. Also, the information from the college application needs to be compared with the DIVERSITY UNIT application in terms of consistency for student educational objective. If students have a change in educational objective, this needs to be clearly stated based on the fact it affects college financial aid, FTE's, long-term planning, education plan, and support services. One way DIVERSITY UNIT is taking steps to address discrepancy in the data is the creation of the online DIVERSITY UNIT application. Having an online DIVERSITY UNIT application will ensure that information from the student collaborates with the information the school has in its databases. This discrepancy also hints about the need for the program to be better informed about how data is stored and how to modify and correct information to provide accurate data.

Educational Plan: The number of DIVERSITY UNIT students with education plans has stayed constant at 84% and 83%. When compared to the college average, significantly more DIVERSITY UNIT students have an educational plan.

The discrepancy between educational plan and educational objective is notable. Students, staff, and counselors need to identify ways to make it clear for students to communicate their educational objective with the school. In addition since DIVERSITY UNIT students have a higher rate of educational plans; this means students need extra support in understanding how to implement their plan. Overall, DIVERSITY UNIT students are more likely than EBC student to have long-term goals and education plans. It is beneficial for students to understand career pathways and have the opportunity for career exploration to put their education to practical use.

Enrollment Status: Most DIVERSITY UNIT students are "Continuing" students followed by "First- time Freshmen." The number of "First-time Student" in DIVERSITY UNIT has decreased from 27% in fall 2003 to 17% in fall 2005, a decrease of 10% points. "Continuing" students also decreased by 5% points in the last five semesters. When compared to the college population, DIVERSITY UNIT students generally reflect the same proportion by enrollment status. (Data for spring 2005 is questionable).

The data indicates that most students in DIVERSITY UNIT and EBC are continuing students. This indicates that the approach to students needs to take into consideration that students have experience with the college and to remedy problematic areas to improve student success.

Units Enrolled: When compared to the college student population, more DIVERSITY UNIT students are enrolled full-time than the general EBC student population.

VIII. PROGRAM PRIORITIES

Based on the program review, there needs to be an addition in staffing in the form of hiring at least one more full-time counselor. Other than that, there is now sufficient staff to implement the program initiatives as outlined above. It is imperative to have a structure for the new initiatives and proper assessment to ensure goals are met.

The need to increase the academic support component is urgent. With the integration of DIVERSITY UNIT tutoring with East Bay College general tutoring services, the result has been that DIVERSITY UNIT cannot provide sufficient access to tutoring services.

There needs to be more academic resources for DIVERSITY UNIT students, as indicated in the DIVERSITY UNIT Success and Retention data charts. Though DIVERSITY UNIT has been very successful in providing the social and financial support of students, DIVERSITY UNIT must plan a strategy to expand on its services to enhance the academic achievement of its students. Several ways that DIVERSITY UNIT is working toward providing additional instructional support include advocating for tutoring services, development of the DIVERSITY UNIT First-Year Experience and supporting learning communities.

Also, it is highly critical for DIVERSITY UNIT staff to have practical training in intervention strategies for at-risk students.

DIVERSITY UNIT also needs to increase its presence on campus though developing cross-department collaborations with various academic departments.

It is also important for DIVERSITY UNIT to improve on-line resources, such as the DIVERSITY UNIT Online Application and its website, in various ways to enhance student participation and improve workflow in the office.

These objectives support the college goals of offering high quality programs and improving the student learning and achievement. As well, these plans follow the strategic plans of the college by improving the image of the college and increasing the number of transfers, degrees, and certificates.

OPERATIONAL PLAN

Objectives	Activities	Desired Outcomes	Lead
Outreach Initiative	High School Workshop Series	Smooth transition from high school to DIVERSITY UNIT	SSIS Coordinator, Outreach
Transfer Initiative	Workshops	Increase transfer rate	SSIS Coordinator, Counselor
Disaggregated Data Collection	Reports on student achievement	Identify specific factors in student success	Research Office
Advisory Board	Planned agendas, meeting minutes	Meet quarterly	DIVERSITY UNIT Staff
Student Learning Outcomes	Develop survey instrument	Conduct assessment and re-evaluate outcomes	Manager

NEW INITIATIVE PLAN

Objectives	Activities	Desired Outcomes	Lead
Hire full-time counselor	Request funds	Approval to hire	Manager
Professional Development	Training in intervention, recruitment, academic support	Improve student achievement and understanding of educational objectives	Manager
HBCU Excursion	Tour HBCU's fall 2007	Funding for 10 DIVERSITY UNIT students	DIVERSITY UNIT Staff
DIVERSITY UNIT First Year Experience	Instructional Support	Comprehensive programming for first year students in DIVERSITY UNIT	Manager
Tutoring Services	Training, additional space, effective tutoring evaluation	Hiring tutors on a consistent basis	Manager
Southern CA Field Trip	Bus trip to Southern CA	Funding for 3 day trip	Manager

Case Study
Student Grievance
and Organization Theory

The students in the Diversity Support program are fed up and they are not going to take it anymore. One of the students named Milagros came up with the idea of a petition. After all, it worked for Milagros's father; he is the head negotiator for a local union in the San Francisco Bay Area. Milagros drafted a demand letter and got twenty eight other students in the Diversity Support program to sign it. The students delivered the petition to the Dean of Counseling, the Vice President, and President of the college along with a copy going to the Chancellor of the community college district. What were the students demanding? No less than my own resignation as the Interim Director of the Diversity Support program.

As newly appointed Interim Director, I had been appointed just six months earlier. It was a one-year term. When I was offered the position, I was told the main focus of responsibility would be to implement an aggressive marketing and outreach program plan to increase accountability in meeting the needs of low income, first-generation students and students of color.

In this chapter I use organizational theory to examine the students' act of resistance that led to the situation detailed above. I will examine the organizational culture of the college, then analyze solutions to the problem outlined in the petition from the student resistance using the organizational culture framework.

Next I will analyze the situation and make recommendations using multiple frames of organizational theory. Finally, I will conclude using a multiple frame analysis of the
college and make recommendations that bring parity between the demands and expectations of the students and my
role as the interim director.

A Profile of Green Valley College

Green Valley College (GVC) is part of a two campus community college district in Northern California. This region
of California has a long history of diversity in the people
who make up the community. Located near Silicon Valley,
the area experienced great economic development and
downturn due to the technology boom and bust that occurred in the late 1990's. Some of the community colleges in
the area were quick to take advantage of business partnerships to create new academic and vocational programs.
Other colleges took advantage of niche markets catering to
re-entry students, life-long learners, and transfer preparation programs. For Green Valley College, the school turned
its focus on the immigrant student population and disen-
franchised populations living on the eastside of the city of
San Jose. The new chancellor of the district was determined
to bring services and programs that reflect the immigrant
community and the diversity of the people. The chancellor
hoped to set the district apart with a focus on social justice,
community engagement, and respect for diversity. The challenge for both colleges in the district was heavy administrative turnover. Green Valley College has had three college
presidents over the last five years. The current president was
not hired by the current chancellor. The vice president of

student services is a hired consultant and a crony of the chancellor. The current dean of counseling is new to her position and was not part of the inner circle of the new chancellor.

The District Chancellor knew that the Diversity Support students would present a challenge for the interim director. Diversity Support students are in a state-funded categorical program that experiences budget cuts and faces threats from state budgets allocations on an annual basis. The students are often heavily involved on campus and in the community. As the interim director of Diversity Support, I began to experience serious conflicts with staff, students in the program, and the Vice President of student services within the first week of my appointment. The Chancellor understood the demands of the Diversity Support program because years ago, it was her first administrative position, she served as the Director of Diversity Support at another community college.

Similar to the district Chancellor, this position was my first administrative position at a community college. The students of the Diversity Support program made an accusation in the petition that they observed me using racial slurs, supporting elitism, and reinforcing institutional classism. The petition was signed by twenty eight students' demanding to remove me from my management position. The students in the Diversity Support program are low income, students of color and must meet academic criteria to be eligible to participate in the program. As the Interim Director, I drew strength from my difficult upbringing, which included being a single mother who is Latina, from a low income immigrant family who was on welfare, single parent upbringing, with a father who served time, and I attended community college after barely graduating from high school. Even so, I managed to attend some of the finest institutions in the country, including completing my master degree at an Ivy League institution. The Chancellor saw me, in my role as the Interim Director, as an emerging leader. One reason she appointed me as the Interim Director, was to serve as a role model for students in the Diversity Support program. As well, one of the main goals of the strategic plan for the district is to stand for social justice and honor students' diverse heritage through the selection of leaders who understand the student perspective.

Green Valley College Organizational Culture

Green Valley College leadership displayed its organizational culture framework in its day-to-day operations. First I will provide an understanding of the term organizational culture and then describe the culture of Green Valley College to provide a context for the analysis of student resistance at Green Valley College. The definition of organizational culture involves multiple concepts. Terms such as the identification of symbols, customs, rituals, climate, practices, values, habits, norms, artifacts, legends, myths, and behavior have all been used to describe elements of organizational culture (Shein, 1993, Cook & Yanow, 1993, Trice & Beyer, 1993, Martin, 2002, Bolman & Deal, 2008). Often the understanding of organizational culture places great importance on the process of the creation of organizational culture in the first place. Who is responsible for the creation of organizational culture and how is it maintained? The role of leadership in the organization is critical in understanding how organizational culture operates (Trice &

Beyer, 1993). Edgar H. Schein provides a definition that I will use for the purpose of this discussion. Schein defines culture of a group as "a pattern of shared basic assumptions" (page 365, 1993). He explains that there are basic assumptions inherent in a group that work toward patterning and integration.

Now that there is an understanding of the term organizational culture, I will explain the culture at Green Valley College. Green Valley College and the administration in the district were operating under the organizational culture framework. One of the ways that the leadership attempted to establish a pattern was through its hiring of equity-minded people to work in the district through the wording and presentation of job announcements. The chancellor of the Green Valley Community College District included a statement for every job announcement in the district:

"We value, honor and respect the multiple cultural traditions represented in our students' heritages. We stand for social justice, and we practice our conviction with kindness, patience, understanding and respect for our elders. We believe that our time-honored traditions are the way to peace. Being a microcosm of the world provides our region and our colleges with a powerful advantage in this new global economy, for the future belongs to those who can comfortably interact and effectively communicate with the peoples of the world. Come share your journey with us. If we succeed, our students shall travel through life displaying human qualities that encourage being tough, yet gentle, humble but bold, while being swayed always by beauty and truth." (GVCCD Administrative Policy) By including the values, practices, and expected

behavior on job announcements, the chancellor established the organizational culture for individuals to as-
similate to or inherently possess. According to Trice and
Beyer (1993) leaders using the organizational culture
framework in the organization must have a dynamic personality and must be able to preach a new vision with
drama. The chancellor was known to make grand decla-
rations during staff meetings, dance at community
fundraisers, and interrupt speakers with demanding
questions and by making critical observations.

The high turnover in the district due to retirements
meant it was important to train potential new members
of the culture of the organization. The manner in which
a new member is socialized reveals assumptions of the
organizational culture (Schein). Before I first began my
role as the interim director, I first met the president of the
college and the dean of counseling while attending the
statewide community college job fair. I met the college
president who gave a full description of the values of the
district and how important social justice and student diversity is to the community and the district. At the first
and second level campus interviews, I met with the chancellor, the vice president, the dean of counseling, the
presidents of the collective bargaining units, and students before being offered the position of interim director
of the Diversity Support program. When I was offered
the position as interim director, I was hired during a time
period when there was also the concurrent hiring of six
deans, two college presidents, two vice presidents, and
a vice chancellor of finance for the district.

In addition to the newly added equity-focused wording on the job announcements, the Chancellor and the

district incorporated structured training to socialize the newly hired leaders in the college administration team. The Chancellor accompanied the new hires on a van tour of the college district to gain a better understanding of the local community. During the summer, the district sponsored a week-long management training institute. In addition, the district and college administration met on a monthly basis for professional development. The Chancellor made it paramount to establish shared assumptions for the new hires in the district. In addition, as a result of the training institute and focused group experiences, the group had enough of a shared history to form a set of shared assumptions that fortified an organizational culture (Schien, 1993). After intensive training and regular meetings with the chancellor, as the interim director, I felt I was working within the shared assumptions of the organization to implement changes to the Diversity Support program to better align with the organizational culture of the leadership.

Analysis of Student Resistance using Organizational Culture

The students were under distress as a result of a changing organizational culture in the Diversity Support program and the college. The change in values, beliefs, rites, and rituals led to a clash in student behavior and expectation of me in my role as the interim director. When I first accepted the role as interim director, I was very intentional in using models of social justice and theories around self-determination in developing new policies to expand student access to funding, to build a comprehensive orientation requirement in collaboration with other student support programs, and designed a whole new student application process, and new program guidelines to underscore student responsibilities and practices within the first six months of my appointment. The previous director for the Diversity Support program had a status quo mentality. Students in the program had little if any academic standards or requirements in order to access direct aid services and incentive awards. A small group of students within the Diversity Support program pretty much ran the show from requesting and receiving grants, to receiving extra gas cards and meal tickets, in addition to working as student workers in the office and therefore had easy access to program supplies for coursework, choice of work assignments and there was little to no expectations from staff nor did the previous Director of the program place any limits on the student workers. The Chancellor hired me as the interim director to demonstrate a new aggressive personality to bring about what Trice and Beyer refer to as revolutionary culture change using accountability and respect for diversity as the foundation for the values to best serve all the students in the program and potential new students (1993).

Solutions using a Single Framework Organizational Culture

The difficulty I faced as the interim director was a result of failing to work in community with enough students in the Diversity Support program to build knowledge around the shifting organizational culture that would have prevented the financial overruns of the program that were underway due to the current lax standards (Trice & Beyer, 1993). The solution then would be to ease student distress by slowing down the cultural shift to accommodate a cumulative culture change, to use change "efforts that are gradual and incremental, but nevertheless cumulate in a comprehensive reshaping of the organization's culture (Trice & Beyer, 1993). The student petition to the college leadership was a clear sign that the student leader, Milagros, felt the need to sew doubt in the new direction of the Diversity Support program. As Trice and Beyer explained, one way to thwart a culture change is to discredit and destroy the existing culture through the elimination of prominent persons representing culture change (1993). Since Milagros had identified herself as a student leader, it would make sense for her to be included in district training and the planning committee to get a better sense of the new direction of the campus. By examining this case of student distress using organizational theory as a framework, the solution would be to slow down the cultural shift to make it more gradual and to include student leaders in espousing new cultural values of the district and involve students with the administrative leadership on campus through training and educational processes.

Analysis using Multiple Organizational Frames

Using multiple organizational theory frameworks will provide a more complete analysis of the students' act of resistance at Green Valley College. Using the theory of organizational culture, the discussion is limited in that the students and I, as the interim director, were at an impasse. For organizational change to last Cook & Yanow refer to organizational learning (1993). The solutions to address the issue of student unrest would mean changing and sustaining cultural meanings that are embedded in the new culture. At the same time the students had immediate concerns regarding basic necessities of life, such as food, transportation, and their membership of a group with their identity as student workers in the Diversity Support program. In addition, my ability as the interim director to perform my day-today roles and responsibilities for financial accountability were at odds as a result of my adherence to the professional expectations for student social justice, which were placed on me under direction of the campus leadership. My authority was being undermined and students were circumventing my position by appealing to the higher up leadership of the college. As well, within the greater context of the organization of the college, it is understandable that a single organizational culture is pervasive to differing degrees based on the size of an organization. Schein explains in his research that with larger organizations, there can be substantial variation among subgroups (1993). Therefore multiple organizational theories are needed to provide a richer understanding for explanations of the students' act of resistance and possible solutions. I demonstrate how the three fames analysis developed by Bolman and Deal (2008) structural, human resources and political to provide a clearer picture of the students and the leadership in this situation.

Structural Frame

The structural framework provided by Bolman and

Deal (2008) explains that organizational problems are usually the result of structural flaws. In this case, reorganizing the structure is a potential remedy. In the case of the student unrest, my authority as the Interim Director was criticized and the students questioned my ability to change the operations of the Diversity Support program at Green Valley College. One possible explanation for these actions, would be that students were rejecting my authority as the Interim Director because they are unaware of the structure of the organization. The students could feel more empowered by understanding that the Diversity Support program is a categorical program and what that means within the college campus. Other colleges choose to have a Dean of Counseling overseeing the Diversity Support program and do not have a dedicated Director. Since the current Dean of Counseling was not well-supported by the leadership (which the students were well aware), the only option was to move the reporting relationship of myself as the interim director to report directly to the Vice President to maintain some authority of the program and to appease the students. The students deserved to be involved in changes to the program policy and included in defining program guidelines for the program. The students, as workers, could also be involved in coordination and developing the focus and direction of the program for it to be successful (Gulick, 2005). By including students in decision making and establishing a higher level of authority (Fayol, 1916/2005) in the reporting relationship, the students would feel empowered and represented in program development.

Human Resource Frame

The human resources frame of organizational culture refers to the organization as a close-knit cohesive unit responsible for meeting the needs of people (Bolman and Deal, 2008). Underlying much of the distress of the Diversity Support students is the fear of losing access to support for their basic needs as students, i.e. food, transportation, and sense of belonging to a group on the college campus. Students in the Diversity Support program are low income and many are single parents accepting county aid to meet the demands of going to college and raising young children. The work of Abraham Maslow and the five basic categories of human needs apply to the understanding of the students' resistance in this case (1943/2005). Students in the Diversity Support program are mainly concerned with having access to meal tickets, gas cards, grant money, and a sense of belonging in the group. When I, as the interim director, made attempts to establish accountability standards that limited access to services, the student reacted swiftly and forcefully. As Bolman and Deal discussed, relationships and participation are key elements of the human resources framework (2008). The relationship between the students and me, in my role as the interim director needed repair. A solution to the problem would need to include reassurance to students that their basic needs continue to be met, even with the changes that I, as the interim director proposed. I, as the interim director would also have benefitted from following the XY theory of dichotomous management detailed by McGregor (1957/2005). By making the human needs of the students' paramount, I as the interim director, would have had the opportunity to validate their concerns and help them feel involved in correcting the situation.

Political Frame

Based on the political theory framework, the students were in a state of distress due to a scarcity of resources and negotiations are a natural process to deal with conflict (Bolman and Deal, 2008). The students' act of resistance exhibited a great amount of power, thanks to the leadership of Milagros and her understanding of negotiation tactics. Rosabeth Moss Kanter explains that those with a sense of agency are able to wield it as a tool for organizational change (1979/2005). The students' sense of agency in this situation made it clear they saw their position as a stakeholder. They defined themselves as influencers in the Diversity Support program as defined my Mintzberg (1983/2005). They saw their role as central to decision making in the program. Using the political frame, there can be an understanding that the students were operating under the notion of self-interest and they recognized the Diversity Support program as their program (Rubin, 1990/2005). The students viewed the program as their resource without any consideration to the idea that I, as the interim director, was as much a stakeholder as they were in the program. In addition, the district, and administration had a stake in the success of the program as well. A possible solution using the political theory framework would have been to involve identifying stakeholders in the Diversity Support program and to build in communications to negotiate changes to policy and practices in the program.

Lessons Learned Using Multiple Frameworks

By utilizing the multiple fames of organizational theory, I discuss lessons learned as a first-time administrator and the matter of students' act of resistance during distress. The various stakeholders, the students, myself as the Interim Director, the Vice President of Students Services, and the district Chancellor, have unique and different perspectives that require multiple and varied solutions. The current organizational cultural framework for making decisions at the college was inappropriate to use with the students in this situation. The administration preferred to use symbolic gestures and grand statements of support. While the organizational culture that the Chancellor was attempting to establish is certainly pervasive and transmitted through the training and new hires to the district in a top-down fashion, the subgroup culture of the Diversity Support program is steeped in activism and community-centered decision making. The students in the Diversity Support program deserved to have a better understanding of the changing environment and there needed to be validation and appreciation of the past practices before any new changes could be implemented (Trice & Beyer, 2005). Using Maslow's understanding of personal needs, the students in this case deserved concrete solutions and reassurances that their basic needs would be met even with major changes to the program (2005). The strength of using the human resources frame to examine the case of the student grievance provides a better understanding of the students' feelings. The most important stakeholders in this example are the students in the Diversity Support program. Using the human resources model, it would be wise to provide a solution of working within the established relationships along with students as well as the higher-up leadership of the campus. Another solution would have been for me, as the Interim Director, to work along with the Vice President to develop a strategy for the students to build better understanding of the position of the college and the position of the students (Bolman and Deal, 2008). In addition, I as the Interim Director, should have built into the program, planning steps to acknowledge the accomplishments and the history of the program at the college (Trice & Beyer, 2005). I should have created a sensible timeline and benchmarks with the leadership that is acceptable given the interim appointment of the position, which was only one year. Finally, by using multiple frames to examine the student grievance at Green Valley College, multiple solutions are evident that would bring about positive results for all the stakeholders grounded in strong social justice and equity values.

State Funding of Diversity Programming at a Community College

A period of change can come from internal, external, or organizational factors that force the college leadership to examine the values of the organization in a whole new way. Currently, the only programs at the community college that focus primarily on the needs of students of color or marginalized students are the state-funded categorical programs. Unfortunately, during lasting economic crisis, the state-funded categorical programs are a prime target for cuts. Many colleges are questioning the purpose of these programs and their financial viability. At City Community College, the leadership had to question the college's values, commitment, and responsibility to serving underrepresented students in order to respond to the cuts to categorical funded programs.

In a time of post-affirmative action and increasing scrutiny on financial accountability, institutions of higher education are hard pressed for ensuring access and success of underrepresented students in higher education. Colleges rely on outreach, retention, and recruitment programs to prepare underrepresented students for college admissions and academic success. At the California community college, there are several state-funded programs designed to improve access and success of underrepresented students. These categorically funded programs include Extended Opportunity Programs and Services (EOPS), Disability Support

Programs (DSP), CalWORKs, and Matriculation. These programs serve a critical role in providing services, instruction, and funding, testing, and personal support for thousands of students that otherwise may not receive a college education. Due to lack of social, financial, and personal capital, underrepresented students account for higher percentages of students on academic probation, fewer numbers of students earning degrees, and fewer numbers of students following credit-granting curriculum (Table 1). The purpose of this chapter is to study the change process of City Community College in response to a cut in state funding to support categorical programs.

The Change Process

The achievement gap of underrepresented students in higher education continues to present a challenge. Concurrently, the student population is shifting toward more nontraditional students attending college; by nontraditional, that term refers to students who are first-in-their-family to attend college and students who are ethnically underrepresented, namely African American, Latino/a, Asian/Pacific Islander, and Native American students; in addition to low income and disabled students. California community colleges offer a variety of retention programs to respond to the needs of these special populations. Retention programs, such as EOPS, DSP, CalWORKs, and matriculation exist to address the achievement gap of nontraditional students. EOPS is geared toward low income, academically underprepared and underrepresented students. DSP is designed to assist students with disabilities. CalWORKs is a program for low-income, single parent students who are receiving cash aid from the county. Matriculation is a program to assist students in the college registration process, including outreach, assessment testing, and college preparation and faculty professional development. In this chapter, I chose to focus on these programs because they received the largest budget cuts in 2009.

These diversity programs came about as a result of passage of the 1964 Civil Rights Act and subsequent calls for affirmative action in higher education on the community college campus. These programs act as the California legislative response to encourage special populations to enroll in community college. All four programs are categorically funded within the state budget. The funded state allocation for these four programs in 2008-2009 was the following: EOPS $2,421,994, DSP $2,611,139, CalWORKs $590,261, and Matriculation $3,130,093. Together, totaling $8,753,487, these categorical programs account for the single greatest source of funding for the college outside the state general apportionment at City Community College (North Orange County Community College District, 2008), Since the 2009 budget process began, there have been calls to cut funding to these programs by as much as 62%. Effective in the year 2010, it is estimated that cuts to EOPS and DSP will be 32% and cuts to Matriculation and CalWORKs were 62% (Community College League of California, 2010). This chapter will be an examination of how City Community College responded to the above cuts to the categorical budgets and how the college supported the work of the four programs, EOPS, DSP, CalWORKs, and Matriculation to maintain outreach, retention, and recruitment of underrepresented students.

City Community College is facing a growing population

of underrepresented students. Holding the designation as both a Hispanic Serving Institute and a Minority Serving Institute, the faculty, staff, and leadership at City Community College must respond to the unique challenges presented by having a majority of underrepresented students. Unfortunately, due to ongoing budget crises, there is the attitude that students of color cost more in support services, and therefore should be allowed to fail, the old "right to fail" attitude (NOCCD, 2009). In addition, there is resistance in using racial criteria in retention programs and earmarked allocation of college resources. This practice of reducing dedicated funding is creating additional hurdles for those working directly with these student populations. Due to state-mandated data collection, the data from EOPS, DSP, CalWORKs, and Matriculation is one of the few methods to collect information of the performance of underrepresented students at City Community College. Because City Community College is due for a categorical site review by the State Chancellor's Office spring 2009, there is data from the City Community College self-report, in addition to personal interviews with those working in the programs.

During the academic year 2008-2009, there were the first rumblings of budget crises on the horizon. The state legislatures failed to pass a state budget for the year and the May revise was late. There was a $24.3 billion budget deficit for the state of California identified in the May Revision in 2009 (Department of Finance, 2009). The NOCCD vice-chancellor of finance and the chancellor began to hold district-wide discussions to alert the campuses that there could be budget shortfalls, especially if categorical programs were reduced in funding. The leadership at the district initiated campus-wide discussion of budget concerns. In October 2008, the district leadership held "coffee breaks with the Chancellor" to review budget issues. At the end of the year in spring 2009, the leadership of the colleges were recommending that the faculty, staff, and students have the opportunity to contribute ideas for budget reductions. The leadership and the chancellor tried to underscore that "people come first," meaning that staff would be saved at all costs.

During the beginning of the 2009-2010 year, faculty, staff, and students were asked to provide budget reduction suggestions during the opening assembly for the fall semester. The college community came up with 401 budget reduction suggestions. Of the suggestions, there was one that was associated with cutting categorical programs. The Business Office of City Community College created a website to update the campus on budget issues in the summer of 2009. During the President's Advisory Committee, there was discussion about possible cuts to the categorical budget. The Community College League of California released ongoing reports with budget updates. It was clear that categorical programs were facing severe cuts, some suggestions were for cuts 32% - 62% along with the recommended elimination of Cal-WORKs.

A policy was introduced in the summer 2009, AB 180, to introduce flexibility into the funding of the programs. The strength of the programs comes from the funding that is restricted to specific programs. AB 180 was a method to disentangle restricted funding specifically for the programs that serve under-served student population. Fortunately the bill did not pass, but the foundation was set to pit one categorical program against another in the political arena.

During the fall 2009 semester, the leadership on the campuses convened to discuss how to allocate resources given the new budget cuts. The Dean of Counseling created a budget sub-committee within the counseling division to address the 62% cut to the Matriculation budget. The Dean of Student Support worked with the faculty, staff, and administration to address the reduction in budget of 32%. The Matriculation and EOPS budgets are responsible to cover the cost of services to students, full-time and part-time workers in several departments, including admissions and records, counseling, assessment center, financial aid, and outreach. The department budgets also funded placement tests and software license programs for student registration.

The cuts to the Matriculation budget resulted in many changes to the operations and functions of the college. All part-time workers funded through the department were released from their positions. The college lost the support of proctors for exams and test taking. The hours of the Assessment Center were reduced. All part-time counselors were reduced or eliminated except for use during high peak times of registration.

The cuts to the EOPS budget resulted in many changes as well. The EOPS program typically served over 1,000 students with book grants, school supplies, counseling appointments, field-trips, workshops, tutoring services, and priority registration dates. The program was reduced to 800 students. Two classified full-time staff were transferred to other positions on campus. One full-time counselor was transferred to the Counseling departments. The annual recognition and celebration events were scaled back or cancelled. In addition, a full-time classified staff transferred to fill a temporary manager position and the position was not filled, leaving a vacancy in staff.

In discussion with faculty, staff, and leadership on the

change process that resulted in the changes listed above, many expressed satisfaction with the level of communication and involvement in the change process. From the district level down to the classified staff who were reassigned to alternative roles on campus, employees appreciated the opportunity to stay in the district. The Board of Trustees of the district provided support for the program after the initial budget cut using backfill funding. One employee expressed the wish that the district had backfilled the department 100% rather than only the temporary backfill. In addition, the employee said that the changes to the program did not affect satisfaction with his position or his satisfaction with the leadership of the campus because there was ongoing dialog and communication about the change process. The leadership of the campus expressed the same gratitude. The Dean of Student Services agreed that there was direct communication from the district that aided in making decisions about the budget cuts. When making the final decision about letting staff go, he received negative feedback from the community. Yet, the Dean reasoned that with the reduction in the number of students being served in the program, there was not the necessary justification to maintaining the previous level of staff. The change process at the college was significant and affected faculty, staff, students, and leadership, yet abundant communication and planning helped to assuage negative feelings at the college.

Social-cognitive Model

The cuts to categorical programs represents a shift in the learning and mental processes of the leaders in higher education. The social-cognition model bases the change on growing, learning, and changing behavior (Person & Miller, 2010). The categorical programs began in 1964 as a response to Civil Rights policy. Leaders in education recognized a need to change their way of thinking about community college students and to provide special funding to support access and opportunity in higher education. The funding for the programs was based on new mental schemes. Therefore, cuts to the program were also based on a change in this mental scheme about serving underrepresented students.

Underrepresented students account for the majority of students enrolled in the retention programs at City Community College. For Latino students in the United States, their numbers are the fastest growing in the public schools (U.S. Census, 2000). Underrepresented students at City Community College represent a growing student population. According to the Pew Hispanic Center's report One-in-Five and Growing Fast: A Profile of Hispanic Public School Students, "the number of Hispanic students in the nation's public schools nearly doubled from 1990 to 2006, accounting for 60% of the total growth in public school enrollments over that period" (Fry & Gonzales, 2008, p. i). The report describes that the U.S. Census Bureau projects that the Hispanic school-age population will increase by 166% by 2050, while the non-Hispanic school-age population will grow by just 4% over this same period. According to the research, 28% of Hispanic students live in poverty, 35% of African American students, and 11% of non-Hispanic white students live in poor households. In terms of language skills, 70% of Hispanic students speak a language other than English at home. In addition, there are students facing immigration issues, such as undocumented students. For these students the prospect of succeeding in higher education is daunting without role models and assistance in understanding higher education system. In Cursed and Blessed: Examining the Socioemotional and Academic Experiences of Undocumented Latina/o Community College Students, Richard Cortes (2008) stated that "Latina/o college students are more likely to experience social rejection, distress, and anxiety" (p. 24) due to challenges associated with their legal status. At City Community College, the categorical programs have trained staff and intervention practices to assist these students to be successful in college.

The ultimate goal of a retention programs is to provide services to at-risk populations in meeting their academic and vocational goals. Unfortunately with the exception of the EOPS program, students involved in the retention program have lower rates for transfer preparation and lower attainment of both degrees and certificates, for example students in the DSP program are transfer directed (that is students who completed transfer-level math and English) and transfer prepared (that is students who complete 60 transferable units with a GPA of 2.0 or greater) at a rate of 12. 92% and 13.1% compared with the City Community College general student population 18.6% and 12.6%. For students in the CalWORKs program, the rates are 11.18% and 19.8% respectively. These high numbers of students who are transfer prepared versus transfer directed indicate that students are taking transfer units and have a suitable GPA, but these students are failing to take transfer-level English courses or transfer-level math courses, which are basic requirements to transfer, regardless of units and GPA. These data indicate the students are accumulating units without transferring to a four-year university. The general student transfer rate at City Community College is 10%, with 12.41% EOPS, 8.9%

DSP, 8.7% CalWORKs. Retention programs provide support for underrepresented students who count on these programs for academic and vocational success. Given the incredible burden of meeting program requirements, it is clear that participation in the program provides an opportunity to equalize the college success rates of students in this population.

Evolution Model

The evolutionary model can apply to this situation because the categorical programs are part of a social system that are diversified, and complex systems that evolve naturally over time as a result of external demand (Person & Miller, 2010). The needs of the underrepresented students are no longer unique to a minority of students. Therefore the reduction of specialized services of the categorical programs can be seen as an evolutionary change reflecting environmental factors.

Categorical programs at City Community College were created as a result of an administrative directive. In addition, these program observe the race-neutral policy in strict adherence with Proposition 209. According to the California Education Code, it is acceptable to use race-focused policy in program policy for categorical retention programs, Title 5 Article 2, Section 56220 Eligibility for Programs and Services, "To date, the only factors approved by the Chancellor's Office are: A. The student is a first generation college student (neither parent has successfully attended college); or B. The student is a member of an underrepresented group targeted by district/college student equity goals; or C. The primary language spoken in the student's home is/was non-

English. D. The student is an emancipated foster youth." Clearly the eligibility requirements for eligibility in the program provide validation that students of color face additional barriers in educational attainment.

These programs are especially important at City Community College in light of preexisting racial tension at the campus. In 2005, the Latino Faculty and Staff Association of City Community College submitted "a Minority Report as a statement of the perceived lack of urgency to address and remedy the causes of historical and institutional inequity that continues to permeate the [City Community College] campus and the district" (Latino Faculty and Staff Association, 2005). There are those in the community around City Community College who have a strong opinion about the leadership at the college. For example, in a letter dated August 27, 2001, the chairperson of Los Amigos of Orange County, Amin David wrote,

The original goal of Title III was to target 60% Latino students in its services and unfortunately, at grant's end, this goal was adjusted by your institution to 25%. Evidently, no effort was made with Title III to target Latino students. This leads our organization to think that Latinos were used to obtain Title III and when received, they were ignored.

The environmental factors that led to the creation of categorical programs in the past have changed significantly over the years. It is clear that providing financial support to categorical programs would underscore the importance of student equity for community members. In addition, there continues to be a need to provide service to underrepresented students, but the environmental factors have changed over time. At City Community College the student population is a plurality, that is traditionally underrepresented students are now part of a plurality in the college and in the local community. Therefore the evolutionary change process model is useful to explore the next steps for the program at the campus.

Multicultural Change Model

The categorical programs at City Community College were developed to address student equity in access and opportunity at the campus. The multicultural change model looks at the relationship between the quality of service and the ability of the organization to function under a social justice orientation for the students of the college (Person, 2010). The programs received support from the district to keep staff and services to students. Yet the cuts to staff and hours of operation will affect students in the long-term. In a time of expanding student demographics of nontraditional students, the college should have shown more commitment to the students to avoid staff transfers and reduction in service. Reductions in categorical programs diminish the development of the college into a multicultural organization.

An argument against supporting categorical programs is that they offer the same academic and social support similarly found in the currently offered, less expensive programs at City Community College, such as the Puente Project. That the programs are duplicating services. It is well documented that the Puente is a project that follows a cultural model that offers a "tri-bridge approach that leads to successful academic outcomes, increased self-esteem, and greater self-confidence for Latino students" (Laden, 1999, p. 180). Categorical programs currently provide programming that is culturally sensitive, culturally focused, and culturally specific. In addition, Puente is a program that follows a validation model in program planning using research that includes validating experiences such as encouragement, affirmation, and support for students in an enabling, confirming, and supportive process (Rendón, 2002). Such a planning model includes culturally sensitive curriculum, activities, personal counseling, and personal mentoring. These components are present in the categorical programs as they currently function at City Community College. Unfortunately the Puente program only serves 30 students on an annual basis; the categorical programs serve about 2,500 students. By reducing capacity of categorical programs at City Community College, this means a detrimental impact to the success of underrepresented and under-served students.

Political Model

In the dialectic/political change process model, the changing role of ideology and belief systems create a conflict that is seen as inherent to human interaction. The change processes demonstrate attributes such as bargaining, consciousness-raising, persuasion, influence, and power and social movements (Person & Miller, 2010). The leaders at the college had to navigate the changes to the budget of the categorical programs using limited resources. Department costs and resources became bargaining chips to make decisions that would align with the dominant perspective of the college. For this reason, the dialectic/political model is useful to provide a strategy to understand the change and to develop a response to the change at hand.

The core mission of the California community college is

to be an open access institution. There are many programs and services that devote institutional resources to targeted populations such as Fine Arts, Athletics, Honors, Basic Skills, Vocational Programs and others. The categorical programs are the only programs that target students with social-cultural characteristics known to impede academic and vocational development. In contradiction to categorical programs, the aforementioned programs are special programs that are not designed with open access in mind. These are programs that instead support a population of student that may or may not have academic or vocational interests that limit enrollment at the college. In speaking with leaders at City Community College, often mentioned is that the college should focus on students who are less expensive to teach, yet there are costly academic programs that are more expensive to provide (such as Fine Arts and Athletics) than others.

Modifications

Modified Political Model

The faculty union and senate leadership at the college mentioned the 50% Law as reason for fear of using operational budget to cover categorical programs during budget shortfalls (Craig & Wilson, 2009). This is an interesting concern because there are often full-time faculty who teach courses that are included in the categorical program budget. This means that covering the salaries of the full-time instructional faculty should not impact the 50% Law in the California Education Code. Therefore a possible solution is to have all full-time instructional faculty in the categorical budget receive funding through the operational budget to allow capacity to fund for non-instructional services provided through the categorical programs.

Modified Social-Cognitive Model

The funding model of the community college system places higher value on the cost of instruction over the cost of student support. Making a change to this value system would require a paradigm shift. A potential solution to the current fiscal crises for categorical programs is the suspension of the Full-time Faculty Obligation (FFO). I spoke with the presidents of the Academic Senate and the United Faculty about the FFO. Both leaders felt that the district office is going to bring the FFO of the district up for consideration. The faculty are prepared to open dialog. They understand it is a concern for the district. As of yet, there has been no honest discussion. If the district was trying to be proactive about the budget problems, then this topic should be under consideration without delay. I think that having more flexibility in the FFO of the district would allow for operational funds to be used to support the work of categorical programs and important service they provide to a very sensitive student population.

Conclusion

The change process of the categorical programs at the college reflect the complexities of understanding an organization with values, beliefs, mental schemes, and behaviors all its own. City Community College must work to find ways to fund categorical retention programs to better serve

underrepresented students. Categorical programs serve underrepresented students at City Community College and the
programs are the only service on campus that take into account the socio-cultural differences in the student population they serve. The programs create pathways for success
for underrepresented students who participate in the programs. Especially when there is a state's economic crisis, the
issue of access and success of underrepresented students
will fall on the leadership to guide the actions of the college.
There needs to be greater attention paid to the unique experiences of students who come to community college, otherwise their failure is on our hands.

Table 1 – City Community College Student Racial Profile

Race	College	Probation	Degree Awarded	Matriculated
African American	3.61%	5.1%	2.3%	2.5%
Asian	21.1%*	14.7%	17.3%	15.21%
Latino	31.3%	40.5%	31.9%	25%
Native American	.7%	.8%	.7%	.7%
White	36%	30.7%	41.8%	46.8%
Unknown	8%	8.2%	6%	9.79%

Institutionalization of Diversity Support at a Community College

The future success of human resource management for any community college district will depend on its ability to consider diversity in hiring, promotions, and staff development. In order to meet the needs of the future workforce in the state of California, the issue of diversity must be present in any conversation that forecasts human resource management. This chapter will focus on the current issues of diversity at City Community College and their impact on human resource management. Using my former workplace, the Cadena Cultural Center, as a site for the discussion, I will highlight how planning can facilitate the recruitment and retention of personnel at the college. The Cadena Cultural Center is a symbol in the college's support of diversity due to its establishment as a response to the critical issues facing the community and the diverse student body of the college. This chapter will also illustrate a process for personnel evaluation to critique the role of diversity in human resource management at City Community College.

Culture of Diversity in Higher Education

Diversity in Higher Education

The history of diversity in higher education is fraught with issues of exclusion, division, confrontation, and overcompensation. The formation of women's colleges, black colleges, and diverse religious institutions, grew out of fervent leadership interested in serving students that were excluded from traditional colleges and universities (Thelin, 2004). The formation of specialized colleges offered an opportunity for woman and people of color to have professional roles in positions on the college campus as administration, faculty, and in management. With the addition of these colleges, a new population of professionals had access to careers in higher education. Unfortunately, these specialized colleges diverted efforts to incorporate a value for diversity. The newly formed campuses were segregated, as sanctioned by the 1896 *Plessy vs Ferguson* case, which established the doctrine of "separate but equal." Later, the question of open access and affordability came under scrutiny with the 1946 Truman Commission report (Thelin, 2004). Racial segregation ended with 1954 case of *Brown vs the Board of Education of Topeka, Kansas*. According to Arthur Levine, in the 1960s and during the civil rights movement, many leaders discussed the need to admit and hire more minority students, staff, and faculty. Policymakers reacted with affirmative action and equal opportunity policies. In the 1970s there was gaining momentum for support and retention of minority populations. In 1976, *Bakke vs State of California* established the use of race in admission policy as a "plus" factor. In a reaction to student social movements, there were changes to the curriculum, with the creation of academic departments in Ethnic Studies ("Ethnic Studies," 2008). By the 1990s, these policies faced a backlash as questions around diversity lost public favor. Californians passed Proposition 187 in 1994 and Proposition 209 in 1996. Both pieces of legislation had public education implications that restricted or denied access and hiring practices based on race or immigration status; Proposition 209 effectively ended affirmative action practices on college campuses in California. In a reversal of policy in 2001, California established Assembly Bill 540 offering in-state college fees for students who attended high school in the state, regardless of immigration status. The legacy of diversity continues as new legislation and practices emerge to address diversity on college campuses and in human resource management.

In California, the Master Plan for Higher Education and the Donahoe Higher Education Act of 1960 (Senate Bill 33) led to the formalization of the three-tier public higher education system. Community colleges were designed with the open door admission policy, designed with the fundamental emphasis on access for all. This policy has meant that diversity is the very backbone to survival and innovation for community colleges (Thelin, 2004). Community colleges pride themselves on the diversity of the student population and relevant academic and vocational programming. Though the students at the community college reflect incredible diversity, the staff and faculty have yet to catch up in terms of diversity. Community colleges fill a niche in higher education that is designed to meet the needs of its diverse student population. But with a legacy of confusing and conflicting goals, in what ways do community colleges meet this challenge in human resource management?

Diversity at City Community College

The Cadena Cultural Center was established in 1995 with the procurement of a Title III grant with the U.S. Department of Education. For this chapter, I researched printed archival resource data including the original Title III grant application and subsequent documentation, including meeting

minutes of the Title III steering committee, Cadena Cultural
Center annual reports, student newspaper articles, accreditation reports, information from the student tracking database, and the subsequent Title V grant application. I
conducted personal interviews with personnel currently
employed in the Cadena Cultural Center, and previous employees in the Cadena Cultural Center at City Community
College. In addition, I was the manager of the Cadena Cultural Center and conducted personal interviews with the
central administration at the North Orange County Community College District as well as faculty leaders of United
Faculty and Academic Senate at City Community College.

Diversity in Action

In 1995, City Community College was awarded a Title III
grant of $350,000 for the first year of a five-year funding
package from the U.S. Department of Education (USDOE).
Designated as a Hispanic Serving Institution, the college developed a campus-wide Title III steering committee to address the needs of the growing Latino, first-generation,
English-language-learning students in the Orange County
area. The purpose of USDOE Title III – Strengthening Institutions grant is, "to help institutions to become self-suffi-
cient and expand their capacity to serve low-income
students" (U.S. Department of Education, n.d.a). The student and faculty diversity (See Tables I & II) reveal the demographic environment of the college. The primary activity
proposed to increase student retention and success was the
development and staffing of the Cadena Cultural Center.

In September, 1996 the Cadena Cultural Center, as part
of the Student Services Division, opened its doors to serve

at-risk students at City Community College. As proposed in the Title III grant application, the purpose of the center was to provide faculty and staff development, student mentors, and a technological infrastructure to provide support for student access and retention initiatives. Central components of the Cadena Cultural Center were a three-pronged approach to serving at-risk Latino youth, 1) *Cadena de la Vida* (chain of life) social networking, 2) *Acceso a la Cadena* (access to the chain) transition from non-credit to credit students, and 3) *Alcanzar la Cadena* (to reach the chain) for the first-generation students right out of high school. During the first year of its existence, the Cadena Cultural Center activities included partnerships with faculty and the local community on producing workshops and enrichment experiences such as field trips to museums and single-parent holiday gatherings. The Cadena Cultural Center maintained an advisory board comprised of the original Title III steering committee. Unfortunately, most of the staff of the Cadena Cultural Center worked as part-time and the assignment was considered reassigned time; there were no full-time employees.

Over time, concern grew at City Community College that the Cadena Cultural Center was not available to all the students at the college. In addition, there were questions about the management of the Title III grant. An article in the student newspaper, the *Weekly Hornet*, on September 8, 1998 detailed how the "key participants of HSI Title III grant committee resigned from their positions on the Cadena project due to lack of administrative support." In addition, the same article explained in a rather racist manner the purpose of the Cadena Cultural Center, "this program would offer gang members the chance to take their relationships and use them to pull the students through college." There was no indication in the center activities that identified gang members were a priority population for the center. The article underscored that all students were welcome to use the Center. As for the overall objectives of the Center, there was no evidence to suggest that the mentoring aspect or the faculty and staff development components of the Center were ever launched.

In 2000, after four years, the Cadena Cultural Center was closed as a stand-alone center on campus and it was moved to be co-located along with the Transfer Center in a shared space. The Transfer Center was designed to assist underrepresented and non-traditional aged students in understanding the transfer function at community colleges by offering workshops on understanding transfer requirements and university admissions deadlines. While the Cadena Cultural Center continued to offer workshops for at-risk college students, there was no department budget, illustrating little institutional support. Also, since the two offices were now in one location, the space was renamed the Cadena/Transfer Center.

This new dual-purpose center is now home to the diversity and transfer events on campus. There is no reference to the Cadena Cultural Center, and there is no reference for the Transfer Center, only the Cadena/Transfer Center. In 2001, City Community College applied for a USDOE Title V HSI grant, with no request for additional funding for the Cadena Cultural Center. In the Title V HSI grant application material, the report of prior HSI support stated:

This activity established a Cadena Cultural Center for special needs students, developing community linkages with role models and mentors, developing workshops and seminars on financial aid, culture and self-esteem, peer advocacy, social bridges between credit and non-credit. All of the activity objectives were met and no funds are requested to continue activities from the prior grant. Because the Cadena Cultural Center was enveloped by the Transfer Center, the function as a center for at-risk students lost all collateral as the funding from the Title III grant vanished over time. After the pairing of the Cadena/Transfer Center, many of the offerings that began in the Cadena Cultural Center have been co-opted by other diversity-related student services departments, such as EOPS, Puente, and CalWORKs. The last vestiges of the original proposal to serve at-risk students with the Cadena Cultural Center have all faded away save for the name of the Center, which is now forever commingled along with the Transfer Center. In lieu of its original purpose, the Cadena Cultural Center is now functioning as a cultural awareness center rather than meeting the needs of at-risk students.

Implications on Human Resource Management

The organizational culture at City Community College as it currently stands does not promote the value of diversity (See Appendix). In college documentation, leadership consistently defines the value of diversity as treating everybody the same (Schauerman, 2003). Yet this approach fails to recognize the very system of oppression and history of exclusion that created the underrepresented status of students in higher education in the first place. Where was the institutional responsibility to prevent the evaporation of support for the Cadena Cultural Center?

In the present moment, City Community College is

experiencing significant retirements and turnover in staff. At the campus level, changes in faculty, administration, and staff will offer a new opportunity to instill an organizational culture that places a high value on the issue of diversity. For the Cadena Cultural Center, recently relocated to prime real estate in the new College Center building, and with newly hired management, it is poised to expand the conversation about diversity at City Community College.

As a result of new management and its new location on campus, the Center is in the process of re-establishing its place on campus, yet there is neither institutional input nor expectations. The Center has launched a new website and a calendar of a year-long workshop series aimed at first-generation college students. In addition, the Center completed a book drive and opened the Cadena Cultural Center library, with resources for students interested in Ethnic Studies and cultural studies. Also, working within the association of college cultural centers, the Center is working to create a new mission as the cultural center for the students at City Community College.

Diversity as a value must include the understanding that special populations of students, specifically underrepresented, academically underprepared, and English language learners are entering community college at an unprecedented rate. In the past, this type of change in student demographic has resulted in shifts in curriculum, faculty and staff hiring, policy, and support services.

The current shift in student population and restrictive state regulations that inhibit and curtail policies directed at special populations of students impact organizational culture of City Community College and the value of diversity in strategic planning. One solution has been the designation of City Community College as a Hispanic Serving Institution (HSI), and pursuing federal funding to develop programs to support Latino students, without the exclusion of open access for all. As an HSI, City Community College must take into account the services, support programs, policies, and practices that inhibit student success; this campus-wide analysis should include strategic planning and a deeper understanding of goals for diversity. As history has shown, an institution must respond to the needs of the students and the local community if it is to be successful and in good favor. Currently, two community organizations are questioning the decision-making process at City Community College, and the Faculty Senate distributed a survey questioning the ability of the leadership to support diversity efforts at the college. These are indications the administration needs to improve communication across campus on diversity and other important issues.

The original Title III steering committee began with 80 interested faculty, staff, and administration meeting on a monthly basis. In the end, the Cadena Cultural Center was institutionalized with a staff of only one full-time classified employee and no general operating budget. As shown with the case of the rise and fall of the Cadena Cultural Center, there is little institutional support for diversity at the school. This lack of success indicates that the college does not have a structure to incorporate issues about diversity in a meaningful and sustainable way.

Diversity at City Community College is not a core value and lacks integration in institutional planning. Campus leaders concur that the institutional planning and human resource management of the district is hampered by the allocation of resources (Craig, Doffoney, Hodge, O'Connor,

Williams, Wilson, 2009). Given that community colleges are responsible to serving the needs of a diverse student population and the legacy of the open door policy, it is a huge detriment to operate within an organizational culture that places so little value on diversity. In addition, as history has shown, schools must be responsive to the needs of the environment and the community to survive and evolve. Especially given the state of California's increasing population of first-generation college students and the precarious funding models for community colleges, it behooves colleges to be able to respond to these events in ways that express a true value for diversity at the college campus. The example of the Cadena Cultural Center illustrates the need to establish campus-wide diversity goals and measurements of success.

Due to the recent calls for accountability in higher education with the enforcement of accreditation standards and the implementation of student learning outcomes, the issue of diversity is now included in the analysis. Just as institutions enhance the skills and knowledge in the area of communication, critical thinking, use of technology, citizenship, and global awareness, the value of diversity must also be measured and analyzed in accountability standards. In the arena of human resource management, leadership must understand how to effectively manage and uplift diversity programs and projects (Mathis &Jackson, 2008). Schools must be able to articulate their commitment to diversity and understand how it functions on the campus through various programs and resource allocation, such as in the case of the Cadena Cultural Center at City Community College.

Appendix

Campus Level	City Community College Diversity Symbols	Status	Role
Curriculum	Ethnic Studies	Degree offered, aging faculty	Brings focus to ethnic diversity in academic studies
	Gender Studies	No degree offered	Brings focus to gender issues in academic studies
	MESA	Discontinued	Academic program to support underrepresented students in the fields of math, engineering, and science
	Puente	High turnover in faculty	Academic program to support developmental skills in English with focus on Latino culture
	EOPS	State-funded, no cost to college	Academic program for low-income and underrepresented students
	DSS	State-funded, no cost to college	Academic program for students with learning and physical disabilities
	Multicultural General Education Requirement	Various courses	Courses that bring focus to diversity issues as part of course curriculum
	TAP	Faculty driven, not ethnic-focused	Originally designed for Latino students, currently white majority
Organization	HACU Membership	Discontinued	Brings recognition of college as Hispanic Serving Institution
	Cadena Cultural Center	No department budget, directive	Office on campus to address cultural issues
	Diversity Committee	No reporting relationship to leadership	Group sponsors and plans diversity events
	Director of Diversity position	Mainly compliance officer, not leadership position	Person responsible for addressing diversity issues with administration
	African American Faculty and Staff Assoc.	Small, aging membership	Group of faculty and staff who address issues pertinent to African Americans on campus
	Latino Faculty and Staff Assoc.	Small, aging membership	Group of faculty and staff who address issues pertinent to Latinos on campus
	Gay, Lesbian Increasing the Dialog on Equality (GLIDE)	Small, but active group	Group of faculty and staff who address issues pertinent to sexual orientation on campus
	Title III HIS grant	No integration or minimal institutionalization	USDOE funded grants that address success of Latino students on campus
	Title V HSI grants	No integration or minimal institutionalization	USDOE funded grants that address success of Latino students on campus
Student Services	Festival of Diversity	Lack of focus on diversity issues	Yearly festival that promotes appreciation of diversity
	Cultural Heritage Month	No institutional planning committees	Monthly cultural celebrations of various groups i.e.

			women, Latinos, African American, Asian/Pacific Islanders
	Student Clubs	Lack of participation, heavy bureaucracy, lack of diversity clubs	Student run organizations that receive college funding
Policy	AB540	Little campus dialog	Legislation that provides in-state fees to undocumented students
	DSS/EOPS Priority Registration	Delayed until 2005 through leadership in-action	State education code requirement providing priority registration for EOPS/DSS student

Table I.

Los Angeles Basin Area (including Orange County) Ethnicity

Ethnicity	1990*	2000**
White	49.6%	41.9%
Hispanic	33.1%	39.2%
Black	7.9%	7.1%
Asian	9.3%	11.8%

Table II.

City Community College Full-Time Faculty Demographics in 1994-1995

Ethnicity		Gender	
White	84.6%	Male	60%
Hispanic	5.8%	Female	40%
Asian	5.4%		
Native American	2.3%		
Black	1.5%		
Filipino	0.4%		

Pura Vida in Action
through a Code of Ethics

In recent years, ethics violations have come under intense scrutiny as leaders in various industries such as politics, sports, corporate finance, and higher education have been found to have breached professional standards of conduct with unethical behavior. Unfortunately, it no longer comes as a surprise to read headline news about a politician or sports figure having an extramarital affair or an administrator of a college being accused of fraud, plagiarism (in the case of Harvard University and Stanford University presidents in 2023) or other heinous acts. Leaders are often looked to for strength, direction, and high ethical standards. Yet the public loss of confidence calls to question the personal code of ethics of leaders. These situations make me question the role I have chosen over the course of my career. In this chapter, I provide an overview of a model of ethical identity development for community college leaders. Then, I discuss my own personal code of ethics that I have used in my daily operations as manager in higher education.

Ethical Identity Development

In the area of ethical identity development, higher education leaders are often left with looking toward ethical leadership models in professional development that fail to take into consideration the specific ethical dilemmas unique to community college leadership. Anderson, Harbour, and Davis (2007) provide an overview of development models for community college leaders and specifically the professional ethical identity development of community college leadership. The researchers call for attention to be given to the "need for formal professional ethical identity development initiatives to support community college leaders" (page 62, 2007). In addition, they provide an understanding of ethical development using the framework of Berry's model of acculturation in addition to literature on professional ethical identity by Handelsman, Gottlieb, and Knapp (2005).

Berry's model of acculturation is a psychological response by an individual to an encounter by people from different cultures. The introduction of a new culture, values, beliefs, and ways of knowing cause a paradigm shift that result in two areas of concern for the individual. Firstly, the individual is concerned with maintaining status quo or his or her personal values. Secondly, the individual attempts to reconcile the new values with personal values. The two actions occur at the same time and lead to development of four acculturation strategies: assimilation, separation, integration, or marginalization. In the article, Professional Ethical Identity Development and Community College Leadership, by Anderson, Harbor, and Davis (2007), they explain that "Handelsman et al. developed the professional ethical identity concept based on the psychological acculturation model of Berry" (p. 63). The process of acculturation can be used to understand how new professionals become a part and adapt to a new organization. Handelsman et al. described four responses to the acculturation similar to Berry's model: assimilation, separation, marginalization, and integration. In the next section I will briefly describe each acculturation strategy.

Assimilation is a strategy used when there is less interest in maintaining personal values than in the adoption of new values. It would seem that a new professional would be likely to utilize this strategy as they have not developed their own personal moral code. This is the ethical identity development that distances the individual from a personal sense of right or wrong and embraces the new organizational professional ethics without much examination or reflection.

Someone with a stronger sense of personal values might adopt the separation strategy. This behavior is displayed when a person adheres to their personal values and discounts the new professional values and standards. An individual who gained an ethical perspective from a previous professional culture might use this strategy if they believe their prior standards are the best and refuse to change to the new values.

Marginalization is considered to be "the most problematic acculturation strategy for individuals developing a professional ethical identity" (p. 65). Using this strategy, the individual has neither an interest in maintaining personal values or connecting to the new organization's professional values. The person is considered to be professionally adrift, with weak ties to ethical values and little interest in the new organization's professional ethics.

The fourth and final acculturation strategy is the integration strategy. Using this technique, the individual chooses to retain parts of their own personal values while simultaneously internalizing the moral beliefs and practices of the new organization. There is an integration of the new organization's professional ethical values and acknowledgment of core personal values. Ideally the individual using this strategy would understand that there may be tensions that arise by conflict between their personal values and those of the organization, but that the individual would work to find an integrative approach to reconcile differences in values.

As a manager, and a woman of color who is Latina, working in higher education over the years, I have worked my way up to a leadership position. I began working in the community college sector as a classified employee, as a co-ordinator. The position was a position represented by a col-lective-bargaining in an outstanding college district. I worked on the collective-bargaining negotiations team and worked with management on employment issues. Since the time I first entered the community college sector, I have worked at many community colleges in the state of Califor-nia which has lead me to serve in senior level management positions. Having experienced the vastly different organi-zational values of the various schools, I see my current ac-culturation strategy as the integration strategy. I am able to observe the specific organizational values and practices in any new position and I integrate professional values from the various organizations I have worked over the years. In the next section I will explore in greater detail my personal code of ethics for my work and in daily operations.

Codes of Ethics

The American Association of Community Colleges (AACC) published a recommended code of ethics for CEO's of community colleges in November, 2005. There is a de-scription of a set of core values that is supposed to help fos-ter the ethical standards of an institution. The core values are listed as:

1.) Trust and respect for all individuals, in particular the lived experience of people of color, LGBTQ+, marginalized groups, etc.

2.) Honesty in all actions

3.) Just and fair treatment of all people, especially people of color, LGBTQ+, marginalized groups, etc.

4.) Integrity in all actions

What follows the list of core values, is a list of responsibilities the CEO of the community college has with board members, administration, faculty, and staff, students, other educational institutions, business, civic groups and the community at large, and lastly, there is a list of the rights of the Chief Executive Officer.

In researching this chapter, I came across several personal codes of ethics published by professionals at other colleges and organizations. In my work at other colleges in various college districts, I have seen code of ethics for the organization displayed in various manners.

As I described earlier, I take an integrative approach to my ethical identity development, therefore my personal code of ethics is an integration of personal and professional values, practices, and beliefs that are a product of my personal culture, history, professional development, and sociopolitical background.

Personal Code of Ethics

I understand that there is a need to provide delineation of the personal and professional values that guide my ethical decisions as a person in a leadership position. I acknowledge that I work in a capacity that serves to directly impact the personal, professional, and academic environment of other administrators, faculty, staff, and students. With this in mind, I will articulate my core values, my responsibilities in my position of a college leader, and my commitment to the higher education.

Core Values

1.) Respect for personal differences including race, sex, language, religion, sexual orientation, immigration status, nationality, heritage, culture, and economic status and across unique personal experiences
2.) Trust and faith in the basic goodness of others and the intention to live in the pura vida way
3.) Responsiveness to human suffering, injustice, unnecessary hardship

Responsibilities to Students

4.) I will provide support for student personal growth and development
5.) I will advocate for student causes and policies that are student-focused
6.) I will educate myself on student issues and problems facing students at the community college
7.) I will ask for feedback from students to improve access and opportunity

Responsibilities to Colleagues and Staff

8.) I will share professional knowledge and information to enhance professional development
9.) I will treat colleagues and staff with respect and dignity
10.) I will encourage colleagues and staff to act with highest ethical regard
11.) I will honor the various skills and professional abilities of others
12.) I will work to ensure the confidentiality and trust of others

Commitment to Higher Education

13.) I will serve as a role model and set a positive example of management for the college

14.) I will participate in the educational community

15.) I will work within professional and personal code of ethics in work and in my personal life

16.) I will not commit or condone any unethical or illegal behavior

17.) I will challenge and raise ethical standards to meet student needs

In the above personal code of ethics, I have tried to integrate values from various professional organizations with my own values as a professional committed to working in higher education. In my current position of mid-management, I understand that I have a different impact on the college and students than a CEO or classified position would in a college. Therefore the values and practices are fluid and would change over time, just as I have changed and grown in my perspective of ethical decision making. My aim with this exercise was to articulate how I view the literature on ethical theory to make connections to what I do on a daily basis as a campus leader. Professional ethical identity development is important to a person in a position of leadership but also to anyone who can impact the lives of other people. This exploration has helped me and may help others to better understand personal values and the acculturation of others with whom we work with in a professional capacity.

Focus Group Interview
of Transfer Students of Color

Interviewer: Lily Espinoza

Dr. Lily E. Espinoza (henceforth, LE): The first question is, please describe when you first became conscious of the fact that you wanted to earn a bachelor's degree. And then, when did you make it your personal goal? For me, these were two different things. I always knew I wanted to go to college. But that second part didn't happen until I was at community college. Then I was like, oh I really need to work towards this bachelor's dream. Not just being at college, but this needs to be my goal. Jump in any time. Did you always know you were going to go to college?

STUDENT1 : I personally didn't. It wasn't until my sophomore year, mid-sophomore year, in high school that I started considering the idea of going to college. My original plans were to be a hair stylist. I didn't want to deal with school. But once I saw, I remember the reason I started thinking that is because I got a 4.0 for the first time. And I used to think that was completely unattainable. So mid-sophomore year, once I got that 4.0, that's when the thought started occurring. I wasn't sure how I was going to go about it. I hardly knew anything about the world of college but that's when it started triggering, when I saw that I was capable of something in education in high school.

LE: What about you? When did you first become conscious of the fact that you wanted the bachelor's degree?

STUDENT2: Well, first of all, because I grew up with a learning disability with numbers, it was not discovered until I came to community college. I had a career though. I was able to be a software engineer. I learned everything on the job. But then when the economic crisis was occurring, I lost my job. It was pretty high-level stuff that I used to do out in the field. System implementations across the United States and Europe. When I got laid off, I had time to think about, do I really want to do this anymore? I didn't want to travel. And so I if could do that kind of job, then I can certainly get a degree. But it wasn't until I came here and started working towards my degree that I learned I had a lot of problems with math. I couldn't remember certain long equations and things. It was funny. Some of the stuff, I could get it, but I couldn't remember it. You know you ask me about three weeks later and I would not know how to tell you. So I got tested and that's how I found out I had a learning disability. But all my life, I never planned to go to college because of it. I just didn't think I could do it. I thought that I wasn't able to do it all. Nothing. But then later on in my later life, I figured that I can do this, I can go to college. I could get a degree.

LE: So, it was when you were here at community college?

STUDENT2: Right.

LE: When you thought about a bachelor's?

STUDENT2: Yeah. One of my teachers said, why don't you go get tested and be assessed? So that's what I did and they found I had a learning disability.

LE: How about you?

STUDENT3: I really wanted to go to college. It was something that was important as long as I could remember. I had an older stepsister and stepbrother, and I can remember when I was young, 5 or 6 years old. So, there was quite a bit of an age difference between us, they were already going through high school. But as I was got older, my stepsister, she went to college to UC Riverside. So, then I was like, well I'm going to go to college one day too. My family members and different cousins or different people, my aunts and uncles, I just remember different people saying they graduated from college or they got a diploma. So, I knew when I was young, college was just somewhere down the line. It was still very important that I always do well in school. I can even remember when I was in elementary school, once I started there was always an emphasis on doing well, getting good grades. I understood the importance of wanting to do well.

LE: So, that was sort of the goal you had from school when school started?

STUDENT3: It was always an aspiration to believe that college was part of my future. I don't know if I knew what I was going to study or if it was a bachelor's degree, bachelor's of arts or science but college was always something that was already in my mind that's something that would come up in the future.

LE: Can you talk about how you felt beginning your academic career at a community college? Like how it first felt coming here when you knew you wanted to go to college and you were starting out at the community college.

STUDENT1: I remember originally, so after that sophomore year, I started finding out different ways about how to earn a bachelor's degree. Originally, I had gotten into Cal State Fullerton and Cal State Long Beach and my plan was to go to Long Beach. I had told a lot of friends already, "I think I'm gonna go to Cal State Long Beach." Being a Latina, that was a big accomplishment because it was a university going directly after high school. But after this and all that, there was something that was missing. So, I made the choice to go to community college. And I remember telling my friend, "I'm not going to go to Long Beach anymore. I'm going to go to City Community College" and they're like, "Why?" You know, they just couldn't understand why I would reject an offer at a university and go to a community college. Especially because community college has this negative stereotype that no one graduates— you know that no one moves on from there. People are there for ten years. A lot of people thought that was going to be my path too. I would definitely say that it was humbling to come to a community college. But after some time, it didn't take me that long, maybe a few months and especially after seeing the great opportunities this college offered, I wasn't ashamed of it anymore. I would just say it. Once I was confident about saying it, people thought it was fine. There wasn't any more shame in it anymore.

LE: When you applied to this school, how did you feel?

STUDENT1: When I applied to this school?

LE: Yeah.

STUDENT1: I felt excited because I knew what my goals were. I knew that I wasn't going to stay here for too long. I was just going to do the IGETC pattern and transfer. And I hoped to transfer to UC Berkeley or any UC. To know I had this other chance to go to a UC was exciting for me. But even though other students don't feel that way, that's how I felt because I knew what my goals were.

LE: How about you guys? How did you feel starting at a community college?

STUDENT2: I was excited because I didn't think I could ever go to college or even think about getting a degree because I just felt stupid. Once I got my first A, I thought, I can do this. Then I signed up for a summer school class and it was an accelerated class. It was modern art or something like that. You know because I was already prepared. Or whatever, I'm going to fail, you know? But I passed and got an A. Then I decided to go full-time. My first semester I took 5 classes and 13 or 14 units. I got a 4.0 and ended up on the President's honor roll. From that point on, I felt like I could do anything. Now, I'm going to go for the bachelor's. I'm going to go all the way. I didn't realize that they had certain programs that you could test for initially, placement for English and math and all that. So I took all that. I was even fearful of taking the assessment tests because I thought, oh is this going to prove that I'm incapable of going to community college, but I took them and I did alright. So, I continued and I thought,

I'm not going to let that hold me down. I still continued and went forward. I went for it. I was like, I'm going to go every day, more classes.

LE: What about you? How did it feel starting out here?

STUDENT3: I had a similar experience to her. I wasn't bad academically as a student, even through high school, pretty high GPA. I applied to quite a few of the state schools and out-of-state schools. And I got into quite a few of them. I went high school in Placentia, and the majority of the students that attend there tend to be pretty well off. I would say at least middle-class, upper-middle-class income earners. My dad, he's an engineer, and he earns pretty decent amount of money per year but there is always an issue of how they analyze and what you qualify for with the FAFSA and net income versus you know, your overall income. My dad is the one supporting me, supporting the house, supporting everything. And even though he makes a significant amount per year, it doesn't necessarily mean he has a lot left over all of a sudden for the amount of full tuition. We had been looking at housing and things like that on campus for the UCs. I got into quite a few different UCs, UC Irvine, UC Davis, UC San Diego. All of them are residential. We started looking at overall costs and the FAFSA, everything, and basically I didn't qualify for any help. I qualified to take out a loan and my dad was like, I don't know if he could handle that type of extra financial responsibility. He didn't want me to start going into to debt either. It pushed the idea of one of the state schools. I was like, okay. At my high school there wasn't a lot of advertisement or announcements of other scholarship opportunities or things available to students. I started to look at everything online. My applications we already done, so that was another let down too. Because I was like, even then, that would have been a few thousand. So he said, "Well you can go to the community college and start there."

LE: Who said that?

STUDENT3: Um, my dad.

LE: Your dad mentioned it.

STUDENT3: Yeah, and I was like okay, cause I didn't want to just stop going to school. I knew I still had to go to college. And then at that time, my dad met my step mom, when I was about sixth or seventh grade. And then in high school, I had my rebellious stage. I didn't really get along with my step mom at all. And that made it not comfortable at home, so that was after I graduated high school. I moved in with my grandma who lived pretty much a few blocks away but on the city side. That's when I came here. I was so excited to go to school though. I started taking classes. My dad had already discussed with me but I knew I wanted to do some type of mathematic related program. That's when I got started with engineering. We'd already discussed majors and things like that. We discussed how even if you're at a UC, they never know when classes are impacted in engineering programs. So, I just started here and figured I would do what I needed to do what was necessary to transfer just to do all the course work. But I was excited coming here. One thing that she mentioned, there is some type of a negative connotation for a lot of community colleges. People get into UC and state schools. They tend to think, "People at community colleges, most of them are there because they don't have the grades, or they are re-entry. It couldn't be because they were accepted into one of the higher schools. I mean if you were, why aren't you going there?" And that is a little disheartening because then you go on a campus and okay, there are some people that didn't do well and so that's why they are here. But I'm one that did do well but I just had other road blocks. And so I get into these classes and I'm still able to excel. But I think people sometimes think, "Oh, you were a slacker and so now that's why you're here." That's not at all true in everybody's case.

LE: Yeah, but overall you were happy to be here?

STUDENT3: Yeah, I was happy. I was not going to give up on going to college.

LE: Okay, so then you all felt—it sounds like you were all very confident but did you really feel that you had potential to transfer when you first started?

STUDENT1: I wasn't sure because I wasn't sure if I was going to maintain like straight A's, the GPA necessary to go to Berkeley or to go to any UC. My first semester before I had really received any grades, I was taking my basic math and English. I also enrolled in the Honors Program. I was in 2 of those classes, so I wasn't sure. I mean it's my first time in college, so I'm not sure how it all works. If it's the same as in high school. So my first semester, I wasn't sure. But after my first semester when I went on to my second semester, I started gaining more confidence. Getting the ins and outs of how to do well in college. So I'd say that after my second semester came by and I did even better than in my first, that's when I started to gain confidence.

LE: How about you? Did you feel your potential to transfer was there when you first started?

STUDENT2: In the beginning, yeah, but the more that I tried to repeat math classes and not do very well, I started to lose hope. Until I got in contact with DSS [disability support services]. And even then I took advantage of other programs. They had tutoring and everything. They figured out that I had a learning disability, so at that point Laura was really nice she said, "Cal State Long Beach has a program for people with learning disabilities. You would qualify for that." So I don't know if you've heard of the Stephen Benson Program. She said because I had a perfect 4.0 and everything else and just the math that was missing, she said, "you know, you should go ahead and apply." But before that I went through several counselors. I don't think that they were listening to me necessarily. I even had one that actually told me that, "you know, you can color your hair and style it different if you're worried about your age." It was a male.

LE: What?

STUDENT2: I don't even remember what his name was but I thought, I go "okay." I said, and I'll come back to this stuff. And so I just went to, I eventually came to Juan after talking to Ruth because I had changed a few things and she was so great. She said, "You know what? You've only got 6 units to take and you're done." And you know, once I applied to the

Stephen Benson program, I was still waiting to hear and after that, I got accepted. But you know, I also applied to Cal State Fullerton and Chapman and they accepted me too and I didn't think they would because they don't have the same programs.

LE: We'll talk in a second about the other schools. That's interesting.

STUDENT2: Yeah, they accepted me too.

LE: But your potential, after you figured out the math. Then you were okay, you felt okay? So that was addressed. What about you? What felt like your potential that you had before to start with?

STUDENT3: Yeah, I didn't have anything that discouraged me where I couldn't perform well. Especially after doing pretty consistently through the K-12 system and being able to be accepted right out of high school to like UCs. I mean obviously, I didn't think that I couldn't do it. I had good self-confidence but I also started to work part-time. Then I moved in with my grandma to help pay for things there. I didn't take a whole lot of classes full-time. I was mostly part-time. What I struggled with was I got into engineering, so you have to take physics. I took one physics the first semester. It didn't go so well. So I had to drop that one but everything else was okay, like continuing math or doing any English classes or any other area was fine. I just could not understand the physics. Even other sciences like biology, chemistry, I still did well. Then I started again next semester and I was able to get by with a 'C' for the first one, so I thought okay. And then I talked to my dad again. I was like you know, I signed up for this next one but for the electricity portion and magnetism. I started to see these are where you have to imagine the fields, so this is even less tangible. I said okay I'm dropping it. I told my dad, this is the only thing that's holding me back. He said, "But you need to have it for engineering, what can you do?" That's when I started to switch to a pure math concentration. Then everything started going a lot better, like the way I wanted them to. But I guess just starting out, yeah I was pretty self-confident but I didn't realize that maybe there was certain areas that would change my focus a little bit.

LE: Okay, alright.

STUDENT1: Can I say one thing? I forgot to mention this in my answer, but since I was in that Honors Program, I remember I had that for English and math. There were different people with different majors. It was not specific or anything. And so, I remember being in those classes and being surrounded by other people who were really smart. That made me question my potential also because I felt I was going to be competing with them in the application process. That was a little intimidating my first semester. Then, like I said, second semester I gained more confidence. I just thought I'd add that on there.

LE: Yeah, definitely. Okay, so I think you guys talked about it a little bit but, did you have any specific very positive or very negative experiences in your planning to transfer, like it sounded like you changed your major because of the math. But did you have anything else? Like you had the counselor who said some strange comments to you about your age.

STUDENT1: I felt funny my age joining it but my professor, Professor Lopez, who is very helpful, she says, "Do it anyway," she says, "You know what? It's very good for your transfer and you should get involved in it." And I said "Okay." So I did. But you can't find information on the college website. You have to dig and do searches. Even then, you don't get a lot of hits on Phi Theta Kappa or Alpha Sigma or anything like that. All throughout the college website, it's not updated, so you can't just go boom and find stuff there. And you'll get outdated information. How do I go to the administration and talk to them about why something is missing on my transcript? Or it's too deeply imbedded in there to find it.

LE: So who did you talk to about those things?

STUDENT1: I just figured it out. I would just go call everybody. They would say call this person over here.

LE: Right, just start calling.

STUDENT1: Yeah, or sometimes there's students that would have information. One of these other students, she was a perfect 4.0, she would tell me. You know, I didn't know about Phi Theta Kappa. I didn't know about Honors, I heard about it but I would have liked to join that, if I had known about it. So, I says, "How'd you know?" and she says, "From some other student." A professor that might know about the clubs. Like Latina Leadership Network (LLN). I wanted to do that, but I couldn't find anything about it except through my professor. So, that's my only thing, the resources aren't there for you to physically access. It's not accessible.

LE: Does anybody have anything in like the beginning when they were planning that either got in the way or really helped you out?

STUDENT2: I wanted to say something to continue with that. I didn't really know that we even had an Honors Program either, so that was something that I would definitely have looked into if it'd been more accessible or advertised. Which then I think also leads into the specific clubs that promote high achieving academic students. Because to be honest with you, I don't think it's very well advertised or brought out to students' attention. I would see that there were Honors courses that said 'H' in the catalog, but I didn't even know there was a program. I just figured there was some of those that just gave you that extra on your transcripts. I didn't know there was an actual program with it too. And there are papers that you need. You know, you have to get authorized or they add something special for that. So my experience with that was, I did call a lot of people to get a couple of them. But even though, there were Honors classes, the professors I had, they never mentioned it, "Oh, we have a Phi Theta Kappa or we have Alpha Gamma Sigma. You guys are Honors students. You guys should also be joining our Honors Societies." You know, it should correlate. You know one hand help the other. The only way I found out about Phi Theta Kappa was, I saw one of the posters put up and it said Phi Theta Kappa, International Honors Society. Then I also saw a couple brochures, when I started going into the other offices. But it was really more of a self-motivated search. It wasn't anything that someone brought up to me. And they should specifically be targeting them if they have the Honors classes right there, cause you already have to have high GPA requirements to even qualify. And then with Alpha Gamma Sigma, I found out because I took Professor Sanchez who is the faculty adviser for that. And he does a very good job though, with advertising it. I know Professor Mendez also does a good job with advertising it for Phi Theta Kappa. However, if you don't have those professors or if it's not happening in some of those Honors classes or just in general for students, how do they know? It was more, mostly students find out either they have that professor that's a faculty adviser or you know, like she said, you have a friend or someone you know very well who is already tied in somehow. Or you have to be very self-motivated to try to find ways to get the information. I don't see that they really advertise it that much.

LE: Okay, alright good. Alright so, now we're going to talk about when it was time for you to do the college search and talk about the process that you went through with that. So think about last fall. So for someone leading up to the last year, when it was time to do the actual application, what motivated you to seek out information about the transfer requirements and how did you first start that process?

STUDENT1: Yeah, like I said I was in DSS. So I was talking to the DSS coordinator. I was telling her it looks like I'm about ready to transfer isn't it? And she said yeah. So I started getting the paperwork prepared and then Professor Lopez, my professor says, "Why don't you apply to other colleges besides Cal State Long Beach?"

LE: Why would you have those conversations with Adela Lopez?

STUDENT1: I took an independent studies course with her because I wanted to focus on additional research. She is fairly limited to certain amount of students. She only takes certain students. It's the ones that are they know they're going to start something and finish. Do a good job at least. She was really helpful in that. She said, "You just never know. 50/50 right? Either they say no or they say yes. So go for it." So I did. I got accepted at Cal State Fullerton and also Chapman. The reason I didn't go to UC was because the situation financially. My husband and I are taking care of my mom. She needs 24-hour care. She's living with us. I can't really say anything about that in records, even though she could never survive on her own. She doesn't qualify as being um,

LE: Dependent, because of her age.

STUDENT1: Right, dependent. And so we couldn't. I wanted to apply to UCLA, but I didn't think that they would accept me. Then another reason, it was so far. And you know, like I said, I probably couldn't afford it. I just didn't think about doing it. Now that I look back, I thought well, cause, I know a lot of my friends that transferred there. But I thought, "Well, maybe next time." Professor Lopez, she says, "Go for your master's there" You know, go to UCI. Because you know, I never entertained it. Because I didn't think I was going to get accepted, even at the other universities. Really.

LE: So, did you know what it took to be accepted to Chapman? You said you applied to Chapman too.

STUDENT1: Yeah.

LE: How did you find that information out? At Chapman, just go online?

STUDENT1: Yeah, I went online and I looked. And I looked at their Sociology program. It was a really good one. And I applied. They accepted me. But they wouldn't give me anything. They gave me a Founder's scholarship, but it wasn't enough to cover. I mean, I was still up to $30,000- $40,000. We just couldn't take that on.

LE: What about you?

STUDENT2: Could you repeat the question?

LE: Yeah, what motivated you to seek out information about transfer admission requirements when it was time to apply?

STUDENT2: Well, I had been looking for information, even the summer before my freshmen year. I took a counseling class and during that time, they gave us some general information. But I remember, I would come here to the Transfer Center during the summer. I found it a really helpful resource. I remember the center staff was the first to talk to me. He asked me where I'd like to transfer. I told him, I mean, I can't believe. It's so funny how I said this but, I said, "I know it's like really out there, but I really want to go to Berkeley." And he just looked at me and said, "Why is that out there? That's totally fine. We have many students who go there. Who transfer there with the right steps." I remember, I picked up all of these things here. I read them through and looked them over. Ever since then, that's how I created my schedule each semester. And before I was going to the counselors every semester. But they wouldn't really help. After a while, I figured they're not telling me anything new. So I found it even more effective to come here or go to one of the walk-in counseling at the Transfer Center. Or look for different resources. So that's how I decided my schedule. And the summer before the fall of last year, I was more thinking of the application. I knew I had to get 15 units to complete the IGETC for this semester, the spring semester of this year. I knew I had to plan that out. Also, really focus on the application itself and take a look at the questions.

LE: What about you, when it was time to find transfer information? Had you been looking since you started here?

STUDENT3: Ever since I started here, I knew there were obviously requirements for transfer, so of course, the method I guess I used to make that possible was my dad. He says, "You need to go to the counseling center. You need to get courses, requirements of what it takes to transfer into engineering." And then, that's when I went to counseling. I made an appointment. Then they give you one of those sheets that's like major specific to what classes that we offer here that transfer for that program. Then they also told me that I need to go to the Transfer Center and get the IGETC pattern, the CSU pattern, a general education pattern to make sure you're fulfilling those area requirements as well. Cause you need to have that in order to transfer also. So I did that too. When I first started out in my classes, most of them were to fulfill the transfer in the major pattern. Then I would add in one or two of the GE requirements. I would do my schedule every semester that way. And then when I decided to change from engineering to math, I started looking where there was changes in that. Obviously, the science requirement changed, cause for engineering they would focus more on doing the science requirement for physics. With math, you can still do physics but I didn't want to do that. So they have chemistry options. And biology options. Then I would see what I would take. I would always try to look also for things that double counted, so that way you weren't spending as much time extra on unnecessary classes. After I got counseling, I thought, "Oh, I can do this on my own." So, the first year to like a year and a half, then I went to summer school. I didn't go back to a counselor. I didn't really see what their purpose was after a year. I just need the sheets. I can do this on my own. What am I going to do? Walk in there and have them say, "You should be taking this"? I can read that. But then after meeting with some professors, you start to see your building more relationships and things like that. Admissions and records staff are like, "You need to talk to your counselor. She'll be helping you get ready for transfer." And then the Transfer Center staff says, "You should make an appointment with a counselor because you need to make sure that you have all the requirements. They can look over everything. To let you know if there's something missing." Then you're hearing from more and more people that it is a good idea to at least meet once a semester, regularly with a counselor because they could be changes or there could be something missing. And then they could usually get more up to date information as things change with the school systems, applications, and transfer. So I said, "Okay." I started meeting with a counselor. When I did volunteer work over the summer, I realized which I didn't know, I like doing math. I never thought about it before. I always thought of math, as being a math professor. I mean, a math professor at the university level. I thought of math as a doctorate. I didn't want to do that. So when I started getting more prepared, more of the general idea of becoming a teacher came more into play. The counselor pointed out all my math. They said that maybe I should be a math teacher at the high school level. I was like, "Oh, duh, I never thought of that." Like I have teachers all throughout the system. I never thought of just being a teacher, just the regular K-12 system. And he says, "Yeah, you would almost be grabbed from every angle because people are so desperate for those teachers. Math and science are so highly needed. You would be great. So many people would kill to have all that math taken and be able to do that." So, I spent a little bit longer here, getting some of the child development courses and units also ready. Then when I knew I wanted to transfer, that's also when I started to get more involved with campus. Like clubs, organizations and running for offices. They were the ones saying, "Oh you know, before you transfer meet with a counselor. Make sure you get GE certified. You know, we talked about when certain deadlines are and coming in here and giving me more information in counseling. I knew when we were going to have campus tours. It felt like cat and mouse. I was just grabbing as much as I could. Everything I needed. Scholarships, financial aid, every opportunity. Like she said, she came and was grabbing papers from every corner, which is what helped me out and that's what I started to do. Looking at different things to try to make sure I had everything in line.

LE: Okay, so then let's see, how did you decide where to apply when it came time to do the application? How did you decide on which schools?

STUDENT1: Well, like I said I had followed the IGETC pattern. I knew it was definitely going to be UCs. I decided because I knew I really wanted to apply to Berkeley. I kept saying that but I mean it's true and then I figured I'd apply to at least 3 more because it wasn't guaranteed that I was going to get in. And then I knew that there was the TAG agreement that we could do through here. So I was like, well if I don't get into Berkeley, I at least want to be secure in other schools. So I decided based on that and also on the region because I was really interested in moving to Northern California. So that was a big factor.

LE: What about you? How did you decide? Cause you said you applied to Chapman so how did you...

STUDENT2: Yeah, as far as looking at their social sciences program, I felt it was a really good one. And then Cal State Fullerton and Cal State Long Beach both had a Chicano/Ethnic Studies program. I think that because of the learning disability, I had a better chance of getting into Cal State Long Beach through that program. I don't even remember what the figures were, but I was one of the first people to be accepted because there was a lot of other people that applied for it. So that's why I went. They have a really good program there. Like I said, several tenured professors. I don't think they do anymore. Cal State Fullerton. I'm not sure what's going on with their Chicano Studies program. Yeah, it was a little bit more welcoming at Cal State Long Beach. And even the advisers are really great too. So, that's why I made the choice to go there.

LE: How did you decided where you were going to apply?

STUDENT3: When I started here. I think I came with the whole mindset of, I was just going to do what I need to transfer. A lot of the work for the CSU or UC pretty much overlaps as far as the GE. I think one of the only major differences, CSUs require the speech component but I mean as far as doing engineering or doing math even, it was pretty much the same. I knew I was pretty set. That's why I didn't even take the speech course until over the summer over a year ago. But my living situation. What happened that made me change from being UC gung-ho to Cal State was about two to two and a half years ago, my living situation changed. I found that I wasn't really in a position now to be able to do a UC. If I did it, I pretty much would have to find campus housing again. I didn't think that it would be feasible to afford all the gas from commuting. Then I was thinking, well maybe I can still do it. And then, the more and more I thought about it, the extra financial costs, even though now I did have quite a few scholarships in financial aid. I was getting scholarships because of different achievements that I had. It still wasn't well compared to the overall cost. It wasn't enough in terms of the UC versus Cal State. I was still thinking, it was more of a UCLA dream.

LE: So did you apply there or no?

STUDENT3: You know what, I didn't. When it came down to it. I didn't even apply to those schools because it would have been like, yeah, I probably would have got in. Probably get into Berkeley. Other people I knew got accepted in Honors. I had an even a higher GPA then some of them. They were getting in. And they were even getting in to, I want to say, regular or other impacted majors to English, you know, not even programs like, "yeah, yeah, yeah we'll take you" such as like engineering and math. Certain areas that don't really have a lot of demand on the program. So, it was like, oh, it sucks. I don't want to be accepted and already know I have to turn it down, so I just focused on doing what I knew I could. Which was pretty much going to be Cal State Fullerton. And so that's where I applied and just focused on that.

LE: Because of the costs.

STUDENT3: Well costs and living situation, I was not in a position where I could do on campus housing. I would have to be commuting. And so that added on extra, me needing to have money for the gas. And if I wanted to do LA. I mean, I really wanted to go to LA.

LE: But you didn't think it was worth it to get loans?

STUDENT3: Yeah, I just, well, yeah. I was already really low income. So, yeah. I didn't want to have loans. Even though they say, you can defer them until you graduate. It's just knowing, it's there. I don't like that. And even with, like I said, I did pretty well with scholarships and financial aid award with FAFSA because I had an expected family contribution of 0, so I mean they gave me a significant package but just comparing it to how much it would take away from my overall cost at a Cal State and then how much it would cost at UC, you still have to add costs for gas and things like that. You know, extra necessities I was like, I can't. You know, it was just, everything was pointing me to where you need to go to Cal State Fullerton.

LE: So, you applied to one school?

STUDENT3: Yeah.

LE: Alright, so did any of you go visit any universities before you applied? Like to explore the campus?

STUDENT1: I just went on my own.

LE: Where did you go?

STUDENT1: I went to Cal State Fullerton. And then I went to Chapman. One of my friends just graduated from there. He was trying to get me to come because Chapman is going through this, they're trying to recruit from the Latino community. I went just looking around and I thought, "Beautiful campus." I was just going to Cal State Long Beach. I drove down there. I just went to one of the Indian pow wows down there. I stuck around afterward on campus. I thought, "Yeah, I'm going to go here." You know, and I did my own little tours. I took a map out on the internet downloaded and just walked around the campus. To do the tour on the orientation day, oh my God!

LE: An hour at those.

STUDENT1: Yeah, like 3 or 4 hours. It's a whole day thing.

LE: Did you guys go visit anywhere where you applied?

STUDENT2: Yeah, I did. Well, I remember in my counseling class I had taken the summer before my freshmen year we actually went to visit Chapman University and UCLA. So, it was just like field trips.

LE: What did you feel walking on those campuses? Did you feel like those were your schools?

STUDENT2: Well, the thing is, something that I haven't mentioned that was a really big factor as to why I wanted to go to Berkeley, is that my brother had been there. I had visited the campus. I mean, not a formal tour but a small tour from him. So I think there is something really special about Berkeley. It was hard to find that on other campuses because it was different like most personal experiences that I have. I mean I thought that UCLA was beautiful, but I wasn't sure if I could see myself there. And then Chapman was really nice too, but I wasn't really looking into private schools. After that, I did the Northern California tour with the Transfer Center. That was really great because I had in mind to apply to Davis and to Santa Cruz but I had never visited those campuses, so I got the opportunity to visit those. And Berkeley I had already seen, so that was really interesting because I was really considering Davis but after visiting the campus I was like, now I don't know. I actually thought Santa Cruz was nicer. So I did and I applied to Berkeley, Davis, and Santa Cruz, which I had visited. And I also applied to San Diego, which I had never visited but I just applied to it because I felt like I should apply to some school in Southern California. Didn't apply to UCLA though but yeah. I did visit most of the campuses.

LE: Did you go visit before you applied or had you ever gone?

STUDENT3: When I was getting ready before graduating my senior year of high school, during Easter, that spring break, I used that week to go up north with my dad and step mom. We did visit a lot of the northern campuses, Berkeley, Davis and Santa Cruz. One thing that I do have to say is that Northern California definitely is more beautiful and warm. Like nature and trees and clear skies. Our campuses have very smog-polluted air. So I know they are very nice campuses. They are beautiful. Even before I think it was finalized that I could even afford everything. I don't know if I felt like I saw myself there at that time. Again, I was younger. I just thought, I'm going to college. I have to make it work wherever I go. Even before the whole UC, Cal State thing, I did think about private schools, because even more than UCLA, I think I was more at USC, like in my heart. Then UCLA came later when I was starting to narrow it down. Because I was like, "Oh, my gosh, there's no way." Because like USC, costs, yeah—that was a big cost. I was like, "Okay, that's just not going to happen." Now I'm looking at UCs and Cal States. Then even with the living situation changing, I started taking out the UC portion. Then it was Cal States and then Cal State Fullerton. I did do one of their campus tours. Me and my dad went. Even though it's local. I drove by it quite a bit. I never really explored the campus. And I thought, you know it is good if I do take a tour even though it's local. You know have them show me different areas and start getting to know my campus.

And when I got there, I was really excited because I was going to be in the program. I knew I was going to be getting accepted somewhere. I knew, okay this is what's going to work for me. And I'm happy to still be living my dream of college. You know, the campus is pretty nice. I was trying to think man, this is a lot more of a walk than City Community College. But I started learning, since most of your classes are upper division, most of your classes now are in just one building or two buildings you're not doing like a GE, where you might be taking the whole campus tour every day for classes. Then they start showing certain centers where there are different things like the library. And then I just thought, "Wow, I'm kind of excited." Now, just moving on. And I did start to see myself, like, "Wow I'm going to be here in the fall!" I was getting even more excited now knowing that it was going to be upper division and university. I think you know, once you know the school, like she said, you get a certain feeling when you're there. You are very excited then. That becomes your school. It's in your heart. It's in your mindset, all of a sudden. It's getting things like, "Okay I'm getting ready to be a Titan." And I started joining some of the Cal State Fullerton groups. I went to the website. You know, like the person at Cal State Fullerton clubs and the different e-mail notifications, like the Titans Student Center. I signed up on that email list already. But yeah, I started out within the campus tour, like the whole lifestyle orientation to campus.

STUDENT2: I still can't get used to the Long Beach State Dirt bags. Dirt bags? Like where did that come from? I have to look it up though. I can't see myself wearing a sweatshirt that says 'dirt bag' on it though.

LE: I didn't know that, that's funny. Okay, so let's see. Now I'm going to talk about college selection process. And after you decided on where you were going to go. Let's see, okay so describe how the application process made you feel about yourself as a student. After you were done, how did it make you feel about what you can do?

STUDENT1: I felt like a load was off of my shoulders. I remember throughout the application process, it was so hard to write an essay about yourself without saying, "I'm this and I'm that," you know. Making it creative. So after I did that, I just felt like what I was aiming for here, was done. Like, that's it. Now it's out my hands. Like my job is to get good grades from here in this fall semester and that's it. You know, continue to do my best. It was just, "Oh my gosh," I felt so much more accomplished. Because I knew that my grades from then on were not going to be as much pressure as throughout those one and a half years. So yeah, I felt accomplished, but it still depended a lot on what the results were going to be. Once I got the results, I felt a greater sense of accomplishment personally.

LE: What about you guys, how did you feel after you applied?

STUDENT2: Relief but still apprehensive because I was wondering if anybody would take me. It's just the waiting and the waiting. But I felt good that I'd gone as far as I had.

I grew up with the fear of education I had from elementary school. I was placed in all remedial classes even, with some retarded kids. With a lot of kids that were acting out. They were smart, but they had a lot of problems. Most of the time I was hiding in the back of the classroom expecting to duck because the teachers they used corporal punishment. They couldn't control the class using words. It was always rulers. Always. And so that reinforced fear of education. So to go from that, to this is, is just another story.

LE: How did you feel? Oh, you replied once.

STUDENT1: Yeah, I was reply number one.

STUDENT3: I would be lying if I didn't say even before applying and now to once I made decisions, that there wasn't any doubt or one lost minute of sleep. That I knew that I'd get into Cal State Fullerton. I even met with your guys' counseling. Cal State Fullerton TEACH counselors here, that could meet with me to do academic advising. I did that a couple of times before my transcripts got sent to UCI but she was looking at me. She was like, "Oh my god, you have everything. You have every course you need. You have it." She goes, "And your GPA is excellent. There would be absolutely no way they won't take you in." And then to be going in to start with mathematics program, she goes, "They're always taking math and science because they need it." So she says, "Yeah, you're in excellent shape." And I was like "Yeah, okay." So even before I applied I was like, "Oh, I'm already going to get in. You know, I'm going to be there." And then she told me, make sure once the application is open, start towards the beginning of October. Don't wait until the last day or the night before or the night its due because she goes, because especially at the Cal State level, there's a possibility with the budget cuts, if for any reason they want to, they can close the window early if there are too many applicants. And also, you don't know if there's going to be a computer problem or unforeseen whatever cause if more people are on, especially at the last moment. You don't want to jeopardize everything like that on just something so you know, menial. So I didn't do anything on the first day, but the second day, I did it online. Got it done. I already knew what I had needed to fill everything out. Once I applied I was like, "Yay!" I'll just wait for my acceptance letter. I mean I don't want to sound like, egocentric, but yeah. You know, I wasn't trying to be pretentious, it was just that, I knew. If I had something like that for a UC level or probably even like a Chapman and really high GPA, really good grades and even having like you know, distinction stuff like that here, then I know that they would be taking me there too. So I wish I could apply and have the opportunity to go to some of those schools but it's a good school. You know what, like you said, there's always a master's, so I have other schools.

LE: Right. Okay, so let's see, what do you think about your selection of your university and how can it effect you later in your life? What do you think that this decision you're making to go to the school you're going to, how can it effect you later? Or have you thought about that?

STUDENT1: I have. Like I mentioned my brother went to Berkeley and he finished his bachelor's. He decided to take a break before going on to graduate school. He's taking a year, well two years off. He says that it's really helpful in any job application to mention that he went to Berkeley. A lot of jobs know that it's a very good quality education. You should be well educated — well rounded. That's something I thought of. I know that I'm going to have to take out some loans too. But for me, I really think it's worth it. And then, at the end, you pay it little by little. I won't have to pay it until I'm done. Ever since my brother's doing it now and I see that he's doing fine. It's really not that burdensome on him. I figure, oh well, I can do it too. And for him, he says that he would have never traded the experience at all. Because the way I see it, is that its way more than just getting that degree. It's a lot more that goes into it. You grow as a person. Depending on where I would choose to go. Because you know every school has its different things I guess. Or just, its different vibe. You learn different things from each one. So yeah, I have considered how it's going to be and the choice that I made.

LE: How about you guys? How do you think your selection of your university can affect you later in life?

STUDENT2: Well, I understand that the prestige factor of going to a school like Berkeley or a Harvard or a Princeton, I'm just glad that I got in, in a way. And I understand that CSULB has a pretty good reputation but like I said, even for myself, I'm the first one in my family to go to college. And so, I'm doing it for my parents too cause they never even got past eighth grade. It's not because they didn't want to, they were poor. They had to work. So in their minds I'm doing this for them too. Not just me but for them as well. I'm just glad to be in.

LE: Wow, and but also you were talking about your Master's program. So that probably won't hurt to be there already.

STUDENT2: Yeah. I don't know about the job situation. I'm hoping—especially at my age. But I'm hoping that in health-care, they have a Latino professionals. It's a healthcare professionals project they call it. And they accept first generation, bilingual students. They have internships that they place them in certain hospitals so that they can become involved in the healthcare administration at the top level. Hopefully, I can get in there but they have a really good success rate with the program. I'm hoping to get in there while I'm at Cal State Long Beach.

LE: What about you? How do you think that going to Cal State Fullerton is going to help you in the future?

STUDENT3: Well, I actually want to say something about prestige. I want to say that yeah, I mean, I know when every-body thinks of Ivy League and Harvard, Penn State, and MI—and you know they even have like Cal Tech or UC Berkeley. I mean, it's really a lot of prestige, but if you look at any UC or Cal State I mean, our schools in California are some of the top ranked in the nation, so I think that the prestige is pretty well established even as it is. You know, there's nothing to stop that. To say that I'm going to one of the California State Universities. Also, especially for me wanting to be a teacher. I started to realize that Cal State Fullerton was a really excellent teaching program, as far as going on to the credentialing. So I'm pretty excited about that. They have a great support system and everything already integrated into everything, as you're doing your major study. So I thought stuff like that was something very promising. And also, what I noticed as far as some of the Cal States, even with their child development service and teaching programs, Cal State Fullerton was one of the schools that whenever there's any technological advances or changes being made or things being updated, they are one of the schools right there doing it first. So I mean, if there's anything to say you staying right ahead of the game or right with everything that's moving forward, they definitely have that going for them. They have that. I started noticing the majority of teachers in Southern California, I think they said it was almost basically somewhere between 60 and 70% got their degree or even higher than that. Got their degrees from Cal State Fullerton. So I was like, "Okay, so that's even better. There is already a lot of great recognition and status associated with getting a Cal State Fullerton bachelor's degree." And also you know, if you want to be a teacher you need to have a bachelor's degree cause it's really necessary for the future, not just for personal fulfillment or like success in life but required to be a teacher and credentialing. So I have a lot riding on this for my future. And you know, I know that I will get a great education, be very prepared for my future. And when I want to look at graduate school, cause I'm already considering getting out with a master's, I think I will be able to apply then to maybe another UC or other dream I had in mind of more money. Even then, like she was saying, if there are loans, I think I would be more willing to take a loan at that point then I am now. Like taking them out. I guess it did help that you had a brother, so you can see it right in front of you, someone who's doing it. Not having that personally, and just being nervous. Like here I am getting into debt and I'm barely getting income right now. There's a lot of things that built that fear. I don't want to do that right now. So you know, we'll see. And then there's more scholarships to be gained once you get ready for that process too. I think I'll be very happy with my choice now. I think I'll be very happy and well prepared for all my plans that come later on.

STUDENT2: I just wanted to add that I am a finalist for the Hispanic Scholarship Fund. I don't, they take forever to process the applications but they sent me letter saying I was one of the finalists but who knows if I'll get it.

LE: Well, good luck. They take a long time. They do. Well, this is one of the last questions. Just two more questions. One thing is overall, if you had to do the application process all over again, is there anything that you would have done differently? I'm not going to ask you because you have like the one school like you thought a lot about the application process. You can say no or yes. Nothing?

STUDENT1: There is. I'm just trying to think. I have a confession. I turned in my application on November 30th. I know that's not that good. I tried in September, to start writing my essay. But because I'm not used to writing about myself, that was really challenging for me. And even though I had a brother who went to a UC, he really was strong for not writing the essay for me. He really wanted me to do the essay on my own. Not that I wanted him to write it for me. But you know, he's my brother, its family come on. Now I can appreciate that, because I think it's good that it all came out of me. But I wish that there was something that I would have just started it during the summer. I felt like a lot more confident throughout November because I remember I would think about it like every day and very often.

LE: Did you stress about it?

STUDENT1: Yeah, in the middle of the night. No, I wasn't obsessed about it, but it was in the back of my mind all the time. During that month, because I hadn't come up with something good. It was already like mid-November. So that was hard. I wish I would have figured out a way to have done it in the summer or that there would have been other programs. I know that the Transfer Center, I would get their calendar. It would say to have the first draft done by this day. But I think that I felt I needed a little more of a push. You know, because you get so distracted. It's still the fall semester. You're still doing assignments for your classes. So if there was a little program that could be offered for students who wanted to be disciplined or to be pushed a little more.

STUDENT2: With the rules then.

STUDENT1: The essay, that was the most challenging part, because all the rest was just basic stuff. Answering questions about yourself, answering things about like grades, parents.

LE: How about you guys? Anything different that you would have done?

STUDENT3: No, but you know what I did see, I did see your email when I came to the Transfer Center. I picked up those calendars all the time you put out. And they had, especially even leading up to the application process within that October and November, I noticed you guys do extended hours.

You were always open late. They always had like a writing workshop at least once a week going on. They even had special things for UC transfer process and workshops to ask any questions. I mean, I saw, one good thing that I want to commend the center on is that you guys do a lot to try to definitely make it available and be more than accommodating to help students during that time. Especially within that deadline, and spending hours and offering even more opportunities but I think that you guys even do it throughout the year. I see like the different workshops and things so, I don't know if a lot of other community colleges are doing that much, but I noticed that your calendars you do is pretty full with a lot of that so it's good to see the support there.

LE: Oh, thank you, I appreciate that. Okay, well last question. Overall, how do you feel about the experience of transferring and your college choice?

STUDENT1: I'm definitely satisfied with it because the dream that I had come true. So I wouldn't have chosen it any other way. Because I saved a lot of money. I also had like different opportunities here. So yeah, I'm extremely satisfied with it. I would definitely encourage anyone who's still indecisive about where they want to go or really has a dream, to come here but there has to be a lot of self-motivation. Especially being from a family that is Latino, my parents just don't know about that stuff. There have been some stress. Even after getting in, just like figuring out finances and stuff. I know of other families who have college funds. Their parents have been saving for them since they were kids. And that's, that's when I would have wished—

STUDENT2: That's not the situation that you have. People are raising those college funds.

STUDENT1: It's true yeah. There are. That's been a little stressful but I'm really thankful that we've been able to figure it out. My parents have been trying to support me in the way that they know how to, you know. And so yeah, right now I'm just really excited for what's to come. I'm really looking forward to what's going to be offered to me over there. I'm definitely very satisfied and grateful that I chose to take this path.

LE: How do you guys feel about overall, the transfer experience and your college choice?

STUDENT2: Oh, I'm excited. I think I made the right choice. I mean, I've already been there a couple times. I took my mom fooling around. And we're up there and here every once in a while when I have to go to something in DSS or talk to a counselor, you know cause I take care of her. I'm like mom, "Look, I'm here, I'm here." And you know, she was at my graduation, so we're all excited.

STUDENT3: Yeah, I'm excited too. I think, given the way that everything was this time in my life, and everything, I definitely made the right choice. I think it was always my goal, to go to college and get the bachelor's degree. Along the way, things happen and details may change, but I never gave up on the dream. And that's meaning that you fulfilled, going to college and getting a degree. I think in the end, anybody who got a degree whether its Cal State or UC, they don't regret the point that all of a sudden. They're just so glad they got it. You don't have to say, oh well I can't get into that one school and then forget it, I mean who does that? You know, so I mean the details can change. You know even when I was in high school I kind of thought I was going right from there to a UC. It turned out I went to community college first. Now I think I have better preparation. I'll be able to adjust better to going to the university lifestyle. I do notice that the retention rate is a lot better more—

LE: The graduation rate?

STUDENT3: What do you call it, when they get in their first year and they have a lot of dropouts? I think the success rate of transfer students is still making it is a lot higher than like incoming freshmen straight from high school.

LE: At the CSU, the transfer students have a higher graduation rate than freshmen who start there.

STUDENT3: Yeah, and so I like that. And also I got some experiences volunteering in certain clubs and organizations and volunteering with different experiences even things like finding, certain, I didn't know we had memorable distinction. Things I would have never been exposed to or gotten if I had not come here first, so I was really grateful for all those extra doors that opened along the way. And you know, if I had to do it all over again, community college from high school, I would recommend to some that it'd be really good to go to community college first. But if they are going to go straight from high school to college, whatever your situation is, just always have a dream of going to college and don't let what comes up, or negative thoughts to be a deterrent to take you away from that journey. You know, you may have to change, change your major, or change the school you were going to go to, but in the end you still get what you want.

LE: That's great. Well guys, those were all the questions that I had for you. Do you have any last thoughts about what this whole experience meant to you all? Or about how this experience is part of your life? About transferring?

STUDENT1: I don't want to go. I love it here. This is like a second home to me. You know, because I had a couple of pitfalls along the way with the math, having to repeat each one twice. I mean, I delayed, it took two years of my time. I thought I'd get in and get out and if I hadn't —if one teacher hadn't cared enough to say, "go get tested" and then have those people help me along the way. With the help, with the friendships that I made with my professors. You know, being able to talk to them at any time. Professor Lopez and center staff had their doors open. They're always there to encourage and I like that. I met a lot of good teachers here. Sad to leave.

STUDENT2: Yeah, I feel it passed by pretty quickly. At the time, sometimes it seems slow but now just in retrospect, I can't believe it. I just finished a summer class. I took it because it was dance and I wanted to learn the music. My last day was yesterday. I had this little time that I had to think like, "Wow. Two years ago I came here and I really didn't know where my future was heading." It's just everything seemed so new, kind of intimidating. It's so interesting now to see freshmen. You know, and to see how they're gonna start their two years. I'm already leaving. Yeah, it sucks to leave, but I'm definitely ready to move on. Cause then I think if I would have stayed another year, then I would have thought, "Oh, I stayed too long."

LE: It is the right time.

STUDENT2: Yeah.

LE: Okay, well with all the questions that I asked you, did you feel that you expressed your transfer experience in an accurate way? Did you get a chance to explain what happened with you during that transfer time?

STUDENT1: Yeah.

LE: Okay. Is there anything that we didn't talk about that you felt was important to the experience of being a transfer student at this community college?

STUDENT1: I think that something that we didn't talk about was more personal stuff like, what other factors could come into play when trying to do two years at community college. Especially for Latinos. We tend to be very family oriented, so you know, what their parents say, and other family members say is really important.

LE: Yeah, we didn't do that in a group because it would be personal. And there would be somethings said that might be hard discussing with others in public. I just worried about that, so probably on the personal side of things I would do that in the individual interviews but the educational research do show the importance of parental involvement. Like you talked a lot about your dad, so we know he's here. And you talked about your brother and we know he's here. And you talked about your mom so she's here. But we didn't go into specific questions about that here but we do know that the family is a major, major factor when it comes to Latinos in transfer. But I wanted to hear from you as your person, as a student here at this college what affected you the most on the college side of the experience. As you were being a student in your classes and out-of-class time. I'll go into detail I think personally, during the one on one interviews. So, I will make sure to include the role of the family in my individual interviews.

The nine individual one-on-one interviews from nine unique transfer students are presented in Espinoza's book entitled *Not Getting Stuck* (Espinoza, 2017) available through Alive Publishing.

Future of Latinidad in Higher Education

In 2024, many Latino students and families are questioning whether a college degree is worth the cost. What if the purpose of higher education went beyond job training and building up your social network? What if the purpose of higher education focused on the healing and health of our nation's most pressing social and cultural problems? The answer lies in the ability of our Latinidad to prosper, which depends on our ability to navigate higher education to build our community wealth, health, and political capital.

For the sake of this discussion, the term Latinidad is intentionally used here with the inclusion of Black and indigenous experiences, to mean a group of people with a shared experience and geopolitical identity that includes the impacts of slavery, voluntary and forced migration, colonialism, imperialism, resistance, race, color, legal status, class, nations, language, forming a diaspora from Latin and South America, and Caribbean lands.

For an abundant future, a radical Latinidad higher education would mean our colleges and universities must be transformed from the individual purpose of human development to the integrated approach of communal and social wellbeing. Taking all that has been gained learning about brain health, neuroscience, epigenetics, psychoneuroimmunology, salutogenesis and health promotion, now is the time to reimagine the role and purpose of our schools and the potential of the self to include our cultural strengths of Latinidad. Even noted education commissioner Earnest L. Boyer has stated there needs to be a "scholarship of integration" across scholarly fields to "respond to the educational and health and urban crises of our day." Today's crises are the mental health and climate crises that are concurrently taking place across our local and global communities.

What might it look like for our colleges and universities to focus on the healing of the mind, body, soul, and Latinidad in an integrative holistic approach to learning? It would mean building a whole new world of learning based on an asset-based approach on well-being, the likes of which has never been seen before.

The ways of learning would shift from the transactional function of earning grade points to wide-ranging holistic practices that support the goal of Eudaimonia or the "good life." Eudaimonia is also described as well-being or being happy due to having a purpose in life. That sense of purpose would provide students the opportunity to make contributions and to be active producers in the world marketplace of ideas.

The current college-going generation sees very little value in attending college given there are all types of knowledge readily available with the tap of a finger on a smart phone. Most colleges and universities only have to offer a piece of paper and a lifetime of college debt. For the next generation of Minecraft players and world builders, only by offering a whole new world of opportunity will they be convinced to join the rest of us in the real world.

Our younger generation come with technical and creative skills like we have never imagined before, with a lifetime of access to the internet. Our schools should be providing wings to students so they can truly fly. The rise of artificial intelligence and chatbots like ChatGPT has proven without a doubt, the last skills young people need to practice in college is regurgitating prior knowledge. If anything, our younger generation needs to learn to be as human as possible. Our schools should be sites that expand our sense of mind, body, and community and self that our students can apply their talents to find solutions to the problems of the world around us.

Using a framework of ten principles for Latino leadership based on work by Juana Bordas, imagine the future of higher education for our community, by our community, and for the future of our Latinidad. What might this look like 50 years from now? Using the ten principles, here are some ideas for how the Latinidad of the future could experience higher education.

Principle 1: Personalismo. The first principle focuses on the personal with Personalismo:,the character of the person. Our Latino cultural belief holds that each person in inherently of value and should be treated with respect. Therefore, the expectation of college can be set for all students in our public education system. Imagine that students received a college registration number (CRN) to be used from the time they begin their education until they enroll in college. This CRN could follow them across state lines and across the nation from pre-K to high school graduation. That way, the student would be able to access records and necessary information that could be stored with the National Student Clearinghouse. Having a CRN would provide a foundation to build trust and respect for the student and a future connection to college, to reach for more and aspire for all that is possible. It would apply no matter their family educational background, language, or other social economic barriers that often take children out of the college pathwayin grades as early as third grade.

Principle 2: Conciencia. Conciencia involves knowing oneself and having personal awareness. Learning about the connection we all have to our personal values, beliefs, and thought processes can happen through intentional in-depth reflection. Before entering the college setting, every student is assessed with the College Conciencia Exploration (CCE) assessment tool on their sense of conciencia, or self-examination, and integration of their values to learn more about their sense of self. Are they optimistic, pessimistic, open minded, rigid, intuitive, judgmental, free spirited, or traditional? By learning more about the personal awareness of students before they enter the college environment, students could be provided with personalized recommendations for courses, programs, and support to help them. This deeper sense of self would help students to develop their motivation and learn more about their intentions and internal dynamics for forward direction and growth.

Principle 3: Destino. The beginning of the college experience should kick-off with a college orientation. The third principle is Destino: personal and collective purpose. Once students have a better understanding of their conciencia, then the student orientation discovers the way destino runs through all parts of life, including chance, fate and the unplanned events that come up for everyone on the journey through college. As there will be challenges, opportunities, and both good and bad experiences, learning and understanding personal destino during the first-year orientation gives students a taste of what is still to come and how they can empower themselves to take on the challenges ahead. The first-year orientation course will prepare students for success by establishing personal and community goals for each entering class.

Principle 4: La Cultura. Going to college takes strength, vision, and leadership. All college students will learn basic leadership skills. The fourth principle is La Cultura, culturally based leadership.Latinidads strengthened by the shared stories of oppression, resistance, colonialism, imperialism, migration, traditions, and language practices. Using the cultural touchstones of proverbs or dichos such as "Mi casa es su casa," the future leaders in our communities gain perspective on their values and heritage by learning from traditional sayings. This link to the past is a connection that will build fortitude for the leaders of tomorrow who must make difficult decisions. These dichos pass down the knowledge from the elders and form a basis of leadership with cultural significance and meaning. For example, the Latino values from the dicho "Mi casa es su casa" highlights the importance of service, humility, and caring for others; these values form the basis for a welcoming community for all people from every walk of life. Every student will complete a leadership practicum that includes 100 hours of paid community service or service learning. Students who have worked in family businesses, they would earn up to 50 hours of community service through credit for prior learning (CPL). As well, the faculty, staff, and administration of the university must be grounded in learning culturally-based leadership as well as part of their professional development to be of service to the students of our Latinidad.

Principle 5: De Colores. The fifth principle is De Colores: Latino inclusiveness and diversity that brings together all the colors of our Latino communities together. The Latino identity is no monolith. Like all the colors of the rainbow, Latino people have multiple native languages, hair types, skin tones, eye shapes, facial features, body types, and ways of being that are as multifaceted as can be imagined. With global migration, climate crises, and changing demographics, the need for inclusiveness and belonging is the basis to generate welcoming communities. Course instruction is based on presenting diverse perspectives that are integrated into the core curriculum with diverse course materials, research, and experiential education that showcase diverse and inclusive perspectives.

Principle 6: Juntos. The importance of the collective health and healing is described in the sixth principle, Juntos, or collective community stewardship. Juntos is based on the notion that the strength from our Latinidad is in the size and sheer number of the many of us together. Leaning into this collective strength, leadership is "dispersed, shared, and reciprocal" across the community. As learned from the leadership style of our migrant resistance, our leaders walk among the people as equals and working side by side with others. The shared history of struggle and oppression has been challenged by the power of the people, (not money). Bringing our collective struggle to the classroom shows the way to achieve the greatest heights in academia. Part of this practice includes the requirement of anti-racist course materials and curriculum practices as well as including students and the community to participate in curriculum planning, evaluation, and program development that is based on democratic participatory models. The birth of many academic fields such as La Raza Studies, Black History, Women's Studies, Gender Studies, and Ethnic Studies programs and such are example of programs born from resistance. The future is where interdisciplinary fields highlight Latino research, contributions, and culturally relevant programming to address the inequities, shortcomings, and overlooked roles of Latinos in higher education. Instead, traditional fields such as STEM, cutting-edge research, exploration, innovation, emerging technologies, and business incubation programs are re-imagined from the perspective of how these content areas directly affect the Latino community.

Principle 7: Adelante! Our Latinidad would not have its full flavor without including the spices from all over the world. The seventh principle is Adelante!, global vision and immigrant spirit. With over 20 countries and territories that make up the Latino community, and connections throughout the world from Philippines to Spain and lands across the Northern and Southern hemisphere Latinos are leaders around the world. Colleges and universities build relationships across the globe, establishing reciprocity agreements to provide all students with access to complete a project in their home country or ancestral home, to deepen connections to their heritage and language. This experience could be an academic term, internship, work experience, or service learning project, Every student is provided with a language immersion program to prepare them for their term abroad; and for students who are undocumented immigrants, university legal services facilitate the passport process and citizenship process to establish dual citizenship for all college students. Once students graduate, they have the choice to remain in the US or work internationally with rights to full citizenship status. Since all colleges in the US and abroad are free of charge, students have no college debt upon graduation.

Principle 8: Si Se Puede. There is an old African proverb that if you want to go fast, go alone, but if you want to go far, go together. The eighth principle is Si Se Puede, coalition and activist leadership. Within higher education there are various systems of colleges, campuses, and types of universities. The Latinidad is stronger with the help of their friends. Many universities are Hispanic Serving Institutions (HSIs) and that means there is an opportunity to build a coalition with other Minority Serving Institutions (MSUs). In the future, HSI and Historically Black Colleges and Universities (HBCUs), and other MSUs have reciprocity agreements to support student admissions, enrollment, and registration. All colleges have agreed to adopt a Common Application for Students of Color (CASC). When a student registers their CRN and they are a student of color, they are automatically registered to receive information and assistance about admissions for all participating institutions. If a student decides to attend a community college first, their application information is automatically rolled over so they do not need to apply to transfer; they receive guaranteed admission once completing community college transfer requirements to all HBCU, HSI, and MSU. As well, to address the faculty and administrative development pipeline, once students have completed their graduate studies and meet minimum qualifications, graduates of color are given priority consideration and affirmative action in hiring for open positions at the participating university systems in hiring. The federal application for financial aid is also automatically completed for all college students using the CRN and all data is pulled from the income tax records of the federal government.

Principle 9: Gozar la Vida. Russian anarchist Emma Goldman is famously attributed with the sentiment, "It's not my revolution if I can't dance to it." The ninth principle is Gozar la Vida: leadership that celebrates life. With the history and experience of the challenges facing many families and communities of migrants with colonialism, slavery, loss, and discrimination, the sweetness of life is important to enjoy. College students deserve to experience life to the fullest and to share in celebration when they reach life's milestones. As colleges all have degree audits to capture academic milestones, there are also career development audits for all college students that highlight experiential education and career development rest stops. As students accept internships, work experiences, study abroad, and other resume-building experience, all are celebrated and recognized at the university with transcript notation and recognition at the campus. A systematic reward system includes free meals, points leading to credit at the campus bookstore, and opportunities to participate in individualized programs such as dinner with your favorite professor or an experience like a field trip to an industry headquarters for the day. The opportunity for family participation and community cross-cultural recognitions is part of university commencement ceremonies. Each campus provides funding for diverse student organizations to learn and share traditional songs, dances, and cultural meals. There is priority funding for cultural student organizations and a campus community kitchen; instruction is provided to celebrate important cultural celebrations throughout the year. These celebrations allow for the student leaders to inspire pride, honor, validation, motivation, personalismo, and distinction from their shared cultural heritage.

Principle 10: Fe y Esperanza. Spirituality is our connection to all life in the cosmos, to all those who have ever lived and to those whose lives are yet to come. It is bigger than the sum of the parts. The final principle is Fe y Esperanza: faith and hope. College students are the leaders of tomorrow. They have a long hard tough row to hoe. They must have faith and hope in themselves and their abilities. College students must learn the role of spirituality in leadership so they can inspire those they will eventually lead. Since many migrants and Latinos come from small business communities, each college student will learn the process to open a small business. They will learn about the permit process, business plan development, becoming eligible for public contracts and grants, and learn how to build a sustainability and succession plan. During the next 50 years, students will be solving global problems that have no current solutions, so every student will be equipped to develop a business plan that produces a viable revenue stream for new college graduates. Each student will be provided with zero-interest student business loans should they chose to open a new business upon graduation. The federal first-time business loan program (FTBL) will make it possible for students to establish themselves in the community of their choice and contribute back to the community while encouraging economic development to address current needs of climate change and social injustice. The FTBL will give priority to social enterprise that address historical discrimination and social injustice for communities of color. With the recognition of the importance of social responsibility, students would have a deeper connection to their academic journey, beyond economic and social interests. With the spiritual connection, more students would be more likely to complete their college degree.

Shifting the goal of education from self-serving to social betterment, that would help to increase the social value of the individual contributions that our students could make in their own future through experiential education, such as apprenticeships, internships, work experience, co-operative education, and international research projects.

In my book, *Nurturing Our Self: During college, everyday life, and the job search* (2022) I discuss the value of transforming our schools into places of nourishing for the mind, body, soul, and the community. For the health of our children and the planet, our schools must integrate the world's best evidence-based knowledge to develop innovative solutions for the well-being of all. Schools could be our salvation, with no time to lose. Let's bring on the good life!

References

Affirmative action. (2009). In *Wikipedia, the free encyclopedia*. Retrieved July 10, 2009 from "http://en.wikipedia.org/wiki/Affirmative_action" American Association of Community Colleges (2005). Recommended code of ethics for CEOs of community colleges. Retrieved March 3, 2010 http://www.aacc.nche.edu/About/Positions/Pages/ps11102005.aspx.

Anderson, S. K., Harbour, C. P., & Davis, T. G. (2007). Professional ethical identity development and community college leadership. In D. Hellmich, Ethical leadership in the community college: Bridging theory and daily practice (pp. 61 - 76). Boston, MA: Anker Publishing Company, Inc.

Bolman, L. G., & Deal, T. E. (2003). *Reframing organizations: Artistry, choice, and leadership* (4th ed.). San Francisco: Jossey-Bass.

Bordas, Juana (2023) Ten Principles of Latino Leadership, https://www.juanabordas.com

Bowen, W. G., & Bok, D. (1998). *The shape of the river: Long-term consequences of considering race in college and university admissions*. New Jersey: Princeton University Press.

California Proposition 209. (2009). In *Wikipedia, the free encyclopedia.* Retrieved July 10, 2009, from "http://en.wikipedia.org/wiki/California_Proposition_209_(1996)"

Collins, K., O'Connell Hodge, K., & Portolan, J.S. (2008). Fullerton College Midterm Report (Accrediting Commission for Community and Junior Colleges Western Association of Schools and Colleges). Fullerton College.

Cook, S. D. N., & Yanow, D. (2005). Culture and organizational learning. In J. M. Shafritz, J. S. Ott, & Y. S. Jang (Eds.), *Classics of organization theory* (6th ed., pp. 368-382). Belmont, CA: Thomson Wadsworth. (Original work published in 1993)

Cortés, R. D. (2008). "Cursed and blessed": Examining the socioemotional and academic experiences of undocumented Latina/o community college students. Dissertation Abstracts International, 69(06).

Craig, D. (2009). Personal interview. Fullerton, CA.

David, A. (2001). Letter to Dr. Michael Viera, President, City Community College. Los Amigos of Orange County. Fullerton, CA.

Doffoney, N. (2009). Personal interview. Anaheim, CA.

Donahoe Higher Education Act of 1960. Senate Bill 33. California.

Dream Act. (2009). In *Wikipedia, the free encyclopedia.* Retrieved July 10, 2009, from "http://en.wikipedia.org/wiki/Dream_Act"

DuBois, T. (2008). Student Services Program Review & Technical Assistance

Equal Opportunity. (2009). In *Wikipedia, the free encyclopedia*. Retrieved July 10, 2009, from "http://en.wikipedia.org/wiki/Equal_opportunity"

Ethnic studies. (2009). In *Wikipedia, the free encyclopedia*. Retrieved July 10, 2009 from "http://en.wikipedia.org/wiki/Ethnic_studies"

Fayol, H. (2005). General principles of management. In J. M. Shafritz, J. S. Ott, & Y. S. Jang (Eds.), *Classics of organization theory* (6th ed., pp. 48-60). Belmont, CA: Thomson Wadsworth. (Original work published in 1916)

Fry, R., & Gonzales, F. (2008). One-in-five and growing fast: A profile of Hispanic public school students. Washington, DC: Pew Hispanic Center.

Fullan, M. G. (2001). Leading in a culture of change. San Francisco: Jossey-Bass.

Fullan, M. G. (2008). The six secrets of change. San Francisco: Jossey-Bass.

Goldstein, L. (2005). College & University Budgeting: An introduction for faculty and academic administrators. Washington, D.C.: National Association of College and University Business Officers.

Gonzalez, C. (1998, September 8). Cadena Cultural Center will help all FC students. *Fullerton College Weekly Hornet*, Volume 78 Number 2.

Grbich, C. (2007). Qualitative data analysis. Thousand Oaks, CA: Sage.

Gulick, L. (2005). Notes on the theory of organization. In J. M. Shafritz, J. S. Ott, & Y. S. Jang (Eds.), *Classics of organization theory* (6th ed., pp. 79-87). Belmont, CA: Thomson Wadsworth. (Original work published in 1937)

Hancock, J. (2003). Personal code of ethics. Elmira College. Retrieved on March 3, 2010.

Hodge, K. (2009). Personal interview. Anaheim, CA.

Hunter, J. (1995) Application for Federal Education Assistance (Title III, HSI). Fullerton College.

Kanter, R. M. (2005). Power failure in management circuits. In J. M. Shafritz, J. S. Ott, & Y. S. Jang (Eds.), *Classics of organization theory* (6th ed., pp. 342-351). Belmont, CA: Thomson Wadsworth. (Original work published in 1979)

Kezar, A. (2001). Understanding and facilitating change in higher education in the 21st century. ERIC Clearinghouse in Higher Education. ED457763. Washington DC: George Washington University.

Laden, B. V. (1999). Celebratory socialization of culturally diverse students through academic programs and support services. In K.M. Shaw, J.R. Valadez, & R. Rhoades (Eds.), Community colleges as cultural context (pp. 173-194). Albany, NY: State University of New York Press.

Levine, A. (2001). National diversity 'think tank' could aid diversity goals [Electronic version]. *Diversity Exchange*.

Lopez, A. (2005). Minority Report – Points of departure (Revised) (Accrediting Commissions for Community and Junior Colleges Western Association of Schools and Colleges). Fullerton College.

Martin, J. (2005). Organizational culture: Pieces of the puzzle. In J. M. Shafritz, J. S. Ott, & Y. S. Jang (Eds.), *Classics of organization theory* (6th ed., pp. 393-414). Belmont, CA: Thomson Wadsworth. (Original work published in 2002)

Maslow, A. H. (2005). A theory of human motivation. In J. M. Shafritz, J. S. Ott, & Y. S. Jang (Eds.), *Classics of organization theory* (6th ed., pp. 167-178). Belmont, CA: Thomson Wadsworth. (Original work published in 1943)

Master Plan for Higher Education, 1960-1974. California.

Mathis, R. & Jackson, J. (2007). Human resource management (12th ed.). Mason: South-Western College Publishing.

McGregor, D. M. (2005). The human side of enterprise. In J. M. Shafritz, J. S. Ott, & Y. S. Jang (Eds.), *Classics of organization theory* (6th ed., pp. 179-184). Belmont, CA: Thomson Wadsworth. (Original work published in 1957)

Mintzberg, H. (2005). The five basic parts of the organization. In J. M. Shafritz, J. S. Ott, & Y. S. Jang (Eds.), *Classics of organization theory* (6th ed., pp. 219-230). Belmont, CA: Thomson Wadsworth. (Original work published in 1979)

O'Connor, A. (2009). Personal interview. Anaheim, CA.

Opposing Viewpoints: Discrimination. Ed. Jacqueline Langwith. Detroit: Greenhaven Press.

Ott, & Y. S. Jang (Eds.), *Classics of organization theory* (6th ed., pp. 368-382). Belmont, CA: Thomson Wadsworth. (Original work published in 1993)

Person, D. R. & Miller, K. (2010). Change in higher education. EDD 630 Class lecture. Fullerton, CA: California State University, Fullerton.

Person, D. R. (2010). Leadership & organizational change. EDD 630 Class lecture. Fullerton, CA: California State University, Fullerton.

Proposition 187. (2009). In *Wikipedia, the free encyclopedia*. Retrieved July 10, 2009 from "http://en.wikipedia.org/wiki/Proposition_187"

Regents of the University of California vs. Bakke, 438 U.S. 265 (1978).

Rendón, L. I. (2002). Community College Puente: A validating model of education. Educational Policy, 16(4), 642-667.

Rubin, P. H. (2005). Managing business transactions. In J. M. Shafritz, J. S. Ott, & Y. S. Jang (Eds.), *Classics of organization theory* (6th ed., pp.280-282). Belmont, CA: Thomson Wadsworth. (Original work published in 1990)

San Jose Evergreen Community College District, 2005. Job announcement on district website. Retrieved March 20, 2009 from www.sjeccd.edu.

Schauerman, S. (2003) Memorandum: Title V Objectives. Fullerton College.

Schein, E. H. (2005). Defining organizational culture. In J. M. Shafritz, J. S. Ott, & Y. S. Jang (Eds.), *Classics of organization theory* (6th ed., pp. 360-367). Belmont, CA: Thomson Wadsworth. (Original work published in 1993)

Site Visit Self-Evaluation. Fullerton, CA: Fullerton College.

Thelin, J. R. (2004). *A History of American Higher Education*. Baltimore and London: Johns Hopkins University Press.

Trice, H. M. & Beyer, J. M. (2005). Changing organizational culture. In J. M. Shafritz, J. S. Ott, & Y. S. Jang (Eds.), *Classics of organization theory* (6th ed., pp. 383-392). Belmont, CA: Thomson Wadsworth. (Original work published in 1993)

U.S. Department of Education. (2009). *Title III Part A programs – Strengthening institutions*. Retrieved July 10, 2009 from "http://www.ed.gov/programs/iduestitle3a/index.html"

U.S. Department of Education. (2009). *Title V – Promoting informed parental choice and innovative programs*. Retrieved July 10, 2009 from http://www.ed.gov/policy/elsec/leg/esea02/pg57.html

VanBeers, E. J. (2001). Personal code of ethics: A living document. Elmira College. Retrieved March 3, 2010 from http://www-distance.syr.edu/edcode.html#values.

Villasenor, D. (2002) Questionnaire (California Council of Cultural Center in Higher Education). Fullerton College.

Ward, C. (2007). Affirmative-Action Programs Are Unnecessary and Discriminatory.

Williams, F. (2008). Proposed Budget and Financial Report. Anaheim, CA: North Orange County Community College District.

Williams, F. (2009). Personal interview. Anaheim, CA.

Wilson, M. (2009). Personal interview. Fullerton, CA.

About the Author

As a professional in higher education. Lily Espinoza has worked at several schools, as well as 2-year and 4-year colleges and universities. Below is a selected list of positions she has held over the last 20 years of service:

Harvard University, Coordinator, University Planned Giving, Alumni Development

Columbia University, Program Assistant, College of Physicians & Surgeons, Office of Minority Affairs

Foothill College, Program Coordinator, Transfer Center

Stanford University, Doctoral Programs Coordinator, School of Education

Diablo Valley College, Instructional/ Student Services Coordinator, Welcome Center, Relations w/Schools,

Los Medanos College, Instructional/Student Services Coordinator, EOPS/CARE/CalWORKs

Evergreen Valley College, Interim Director, EOPS/CARE/CalWORKs

Fullerton College, Director, Cadena Cultural Center & Transfer Center

California State University, Fullerton, Instructor, Student Leadership Institute

Solano College, Dean/Athletic Director, School of Human Performance & Development

Mt. Diablo Unified School District, Substitute Teacher

Mills College, Instructor, Upward Bound (TRIO)

UC Berkeley, Assistant Director, Cal Alumni Association, Berkeley Career Network

UC Davis, Director, Latinx Retention Initiative

California State University, Maritime Academy, Director, Career Services & Industry Relations

Ohlone College, Director, Career Services & Industry Relations

UC Santa Cruz, Asst. Director, Creating Equity in STEAM (CrEST), Science Internship Program (SIP)

ABOOKS

ALIVE Book Publishing and ALIVE Publishing Group
are imprints of Advanced Publishing LLC,
3200 A Danville Blvd., Suite 204, Alamo, California 94507

925.837.7303
alivebookpublishing.com

www.ingramcontent.com/pod-product-compliance
Lightning Source LLC
Chambersburg PA
CBHW031433270326
41930CB00007B/684